Talking With Donkeys
Third Edition

saving them all

Written & Photographed By
Mark S. Meyers

Talking With Donkeys
Saving them all
Third Edition
Copyright 2008 by Peaceful Valley Donkey Rescue, Inc. All rights reserved.

Printed in the United States of America. No part of this book may be reproduced or transmitted in any form or by any means, electronic or mechanical, including photocopying, recording, or by any information storage or retrieval system, without permission from the publisher.

For information, contact:
Peaceful Valley Donkey Rescue, Inc.
PO Box 2210 Tehachapi, CA 93581
Phone 866-DONKS-31
www.donkeyrescue.org

Written by Mark S. Meyers
Book design by Mark S. Meyers
Photographs and Graphic Designs by Mark S. Meyers
Pictures of Mark Meyers taken by Amy Meyers, Mark S. Meyers and the Peaceful Valley Staff. All rights reserved. Copyright 2008

Cover Design by Mark Meyers
Cover Photo by Amy Meyers

ISBN: 978-0-9771471-3-7

First Edition: August 01, 2005
Talking With Donkeys:
An intimate look at the world's most maligned animals
Second Edition: June 01, 2006
Talking With Donkeys:
The simple philosophy of a 21st century burro man
Third Edition: October 01, 2008
Talking With Donkeys:
Saving them all

This book is published by The Peaceful Valley Donkey Rescue in support of its work both nationally and internationally. Proceeds generated from the sale of this book directly support the Peaceful Valley Donkey Rescue.

This book represents the views and opinions of Mark Meyers. If you are offended by any of it's content please feel free to throw it away, give it to someone else, or write your own book. And for everyone's sake, do it quietly.

This book is dedicated to the ones we saved, the ones we lost and the ones that are still out there.

It is dedicated to the memory of my friend Chris Hay.

And it is especially dedicated to my best friend, my lover & my wife Amy

When a person thinks of donkeys, they think of two things: Jackasses and My Dad.

Mark Meyers, my Dad, has left a great print on the art of donkey rescue. He has taught the world a new way to think of the jackass. Not as a put-down, but as a creature with feelings, intelligence and the ability to express love. He has lived, and nearly died, with his beloved donkeys. Through it all, one can learn about the nature of donkeys and what they truly represent.

My Dad lives in Texas and is currently working on a huge project. This has taken him away from our family, but we all agree that the lives saved far outweigh our own needs. Sacrifice and selflessness are two things that my Dad has instilled in all of us. As an adult, I hope that I can be as great a man as my Dad.

Josh Meyers
Age 14

I am only afraid of three things in this world: Heights, Snakes and my Dad.

Heights and snakes speak for themselves, but many people are surprised of why I am afraid of my Dad. It is not his size, strength or appearance, I am afraid of my Dad because I do not want to disappoint him. My Dad had taught all of his children to think for themselves and make the right decisions. If I have disappointed him, then I have made a bad decision.

My Dad is a man of few words, he can say more with a look than most people can say with a mouthful. My Dad is kind of like a safety net, he is always there to protect his family, his few friends, the weak and especially the donkeys. It had been hard not having my Dad around these last few months, but he has taught us how to be strong and how to help our Mom. I hope that one day I will be the same kind of man as my Dad.

Jake Meyers
Age 13

"I built an empire, so that each can have their own throne; I've taken in what was turned away, so that no donkey has to be alone. Neglected, abused, wild, used up, come in and sit down, I offer you my cup. Drink until you are quenched, eat until you are full, life should not be this way, if you must cry, it is you I console."

"Why was my land taken? Why do I wait in vane? Love never given, but you - you are not the same. The energy you bring, breaks apart what days are dark, sunshine through the clouds, and here - this is where love will start."

"No expectations - you will be given everything you need. This is your new beginning, new life that will grow from a seed. So be strong; lift your head high! I am your protector - live life in peace, live your life with pride."

So many donkeys have the fortune of making their way to Peaceful Valley Donkey Rescue. No matter where the location, all of our ranches have the means to heal and revive any broken soul. Mark Meyers has made it his life's path to rescue and rehabilitate donkeys on a national level. His dedication and sacrifice has been selfless with endless amounts of time spent away from his family. The connection and personal relationships he has made with each donkey is astounding! One only wonders how he can keep track of so many different names and personalities. However, that is one of many amazing attributes when it comes to Mark and his family. This is their life, day in and day out. PVDR will always be a success story because they will not allow it to be any other way.

I am proud to be a link in this remarkable chain. I wrote the poem at the top of this page to reflect Mark's mission, a donkey's perspective and Mark's ability to protect and make everything feel safe. In many ways the last paragraph applies to my life as well. Mark has given me the tools to reach deep inside myself and make a difference in everything I do: to live life in peace and live life with pride. Compassion is a profound human emotion prompted by the pain of others and that is one key ingredient in Marks life that you see and feel as you walk through his ranches. He is a protector, savior and healer, a husband, father and friend. It is with great pride, I give you Mr. Mark Meyers.

Devin Kerley
Peaceful Valley Donkey Rescue
Medical Tech/Trainer/Trustee

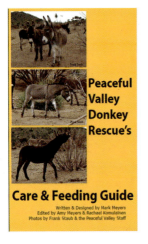

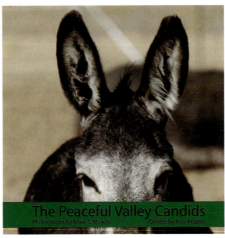

Introduction

I was listening to an interview on a talk radio program the other day in my truck. A man had written a book about his troubled teenage years. His life, during those years, was filled with misery and bad decisions. He had run away at the age of 15. He was addicted to crack cocaine and became a prostitute to pay for his drug habit. He was able, after some years, to pull his life together and clean himself up. The book chronicles his struggles and his victories. Towards the end of the interview, the author made a very common statement. One that I have heard repeated hundreds of times relating to books, movies and other good deeds. The author stated, "This will all be worth it, if I am able to get just one kid off of the streets."

Many things of changed since the release of Talking With Donkeys: The simple philosophy of a 21st Century Burroman. The rescue is now Coast to Coast, and we are still growing. We have facilities in so many states that I hesitate to mention how many because I know that there will be more before this book is printed. We are getting closer to our goal of being able to rescue a donkey from, or adopt a donkey into, any place in the United States of America.

This growth has not come without a price. I have lost many friends, or more accurately, I have found out who my friends really are. I have had to live apart from my family for months at a time. I have traveled thousands of miles by airplane and truck. We have had to "grow up" as a corporation and look at business from a national perspective and not from a local one. We have had to get "lean and mean" in order to build a Rescue unlike anything that has been done before.

It has been more than eight years since I wrote the article "The Plight of the American Donkey". Along with my article "Why Do People Abuse Donkeys" they been republished in more than 30 different publications and translated into four different languages. Our Peaceful Valley Care and Feeding Manual has been distributed to more than 5,000 donkey owners worldwide and we hope to have the Spanish version printed very soon. Talking With Donkeys 1st and 2nd editions combined for more than 4,000 copies sold. Peaceful Valley Candids has sold over 3,500 copies and the Peaceful Valley National Plan book has been requested and distributed to 500 households across the country.

So let me be perfectly clear on this one point. If all of the sum total of my efforts result in only helping one donkey, then I need to find a new line of work. While saving a life is noble, saving a species is crucial. In the future, if you ever hear me say, "This will all be worth it if I am able to save just one donkey" you have my permission to slap me on top of my bald head.

Until the day comes when I can no longer draw breath:

> I will be working towards **SAVING THEM ALL!**

Part 1
DONKEYS

    The hardest part of donkey rescue is convincing people why donkeys are worth saving. This is not an easy task as most people hold a fairly low opinion of our longeared friends. The following pages are filled with stories, some happy and some sad, of the donkeys that have come into my life. I have also included some information on donkeys as well as the outline for the three problems that are faced by donkeys in our nation.

    My goal is not to upset you, but rather to inspire you and to share some of the common problems that donkeys are faced with today. If I can give you a better opinion of donkeys, then perhaps I can count on you as a friend, an ally and a person who will not turn a blind eye to the Plight of the American Donkey.

The American Donkey

As a rescuer of donkeys, I often forget that most people don't know the things that I take for granted. Doctors understand injuries, dentists understand teeth, lawyers understand contracts and I understand donkeys. I have spent so much time with these animals that I can feel what they feel, read their body language and predict their actions. Time has given me perspective, but my breakthrough in understanding came when I finally realized that these are truly noble creatures, each and every one. I have unconditionally accepted them into my life and they have allowed me into their lives.

Will Rogers once said, "I never met a man I didn't like." Few of us in today's fast paced, keepin' up with Jones', super-sized, wireless world, share Mr. Rogers' sentiments about others. I witness the effects of human cruelty on a daily basis and it has made me question the moral authority of humans. I can say without hesitation, however, that I have never met a donkey that I didn't like. Regardless of their background, I have found a loving friend in every donkey that has crossed my path.

Most people view donkeys as hardheaded and stubborn—a stupid animal that was used by lonely old prospectors to carry equipment, possessing little or no use in today's world. After all, where do they fit in? They're not listed on the endangered species list. Chances are, you'll never see one in a pet store between the kittens and puppies. The equine community largely ignores them and the general public doesn't understand them. Since they are typically not counted as a farm animal and are considered feral in the wild, the American Donkey is often worth more dead than alive.

The wild burros of America are a living link to our past. Their character has not changed with time, but time has dramatically changed the character of the land they helped tame. Once the faithful companions to explorers and miners, the era of the donkey in America was brought to an end, in large part, by the steadfast toil of the donkeys themselves. There was no room and little appreciation for them in the world they helped create. Many were simply released into the wild to fend for themselves. I've often wondered how many days, months, even years, it took these loyal animals to understand that they were no longer wanted.

The deserts of Arizona, Nevada, and California were a perfect home for these rugged animals. They managed to keep their breed strong and healthy for many centuries, but human intervention is now taking its toll. Although dams, roads, fences, pollution and power plants are acceptable scars on our natural surroundings, donkeys are viewed as an immediate threat to the environment. As a water-drinking mammal, competition with domestic cattle has resulted in their numbers being dramatically reduced. American wild burros are still being forced from their land and

are at constant risk of being used for target practice.

    Because the thousands of wild donkeys found in the American Southwest originated from domestic donkeys, they are considered feral animals. Protected only on lands administered by the Bureau of Land Management, burros are under constant threat of being shot on other Federal, State and Indian Lands. Some wild burros, as well as domestic donkeys, end up at slaughter plants where they are rendered into dog food or processed for human consumption. Donkey meat is often shipped abroad where it is considered a delicacy in upscale restaurants. What does it tell us about ourselves when we allow a symbol of American strength and independence to be butchered and shipped to foreign lands for consumption?

In 2000, Amy and I turned a back yard hobby into a full fledged, nonprofit charity. In the early days of the rescue, the mission of the organization was to "Provide a safe and loving environment to abused, neglected and unwanted donkeys". This proved to be naïve. While saving an individual donkey is a noble cause, it does little to prevent future misfortunes or to make an overall impact on the plight of donkeys nationwide. For the most part, donkey rescues in this country operate on a limited basis, in a limited area, with limited funding, always helping the individual but not addressing the larger problem. In 2007, I assembled a plan to rescue donkeys on a national level. I am pleased to say that we are well on our way to achieving this dream.

In order to understand the need to build a national rescue, one must understand the problems that donkeys face. Later in this section you will read the individual stories of some of the donkeys in our system. These same stories are repeated all across the country. The following is an explanation of the root causes of these problems.

The Problems

Public Perception

In every human culture from China to Europe and into the America's, the donkey has always been ridiculed and labeled as stubborn. The common ass, or donkey, is the poor man's beast of burden in the third world and has lost its place of value in the industrialized nations of today's fast paced societies. In almost every country, in almost every language, men insult each other with the name "Jackass". In cartoons, the hero transforms into donkey when he acts foolish. When Pinocchio was overindulgent, he became a donkey. An animal must be viewed as having worth before any concerted effort can be made to safeguard them from abuse and neglect. A look into our past is necessary to find the many contributions of the donkey and give credit for its amazing contributions to our culture, the American Culture.

Abuse and neglect at the hands of ignorant owners

Donkey owners fall mainly into two groups, horse people who acquired donkeys and animal novices that thought it would be fun to own donkeys. For clarification, there are many great owners who understand their donkeys and provide exemplary care for them. These responsible owners are not included as part of the problem, but should be counted on as part of the solution.

Horse owners have expectations on their animals. Horses are "broken" in spirit and trained to accept a set of universal commands.

Without question a well trained horse will accept a halter, walk on lead, stand tied and pick up all four hooves. A horse's training is based on their 'flight' instinct and their natural behaviors based on herd dynamics. These same instincts and behaviors are not present in donkeys. In order to gentle and train a donkey it takes an entirely different set of skills, expectations and patience.

The novice owners are not an automatic problem as long as they seek help. We often times find that a novice donkey owner is more apt to not fall into the same trap of expectations that a more experienced horse person might. But it is the novice owner that does not seek council that usually ends up either neglecting the needs of the donkeys within their care or resorts to abuse in order to try and get the results they seek.

Most first time donkey owners, especially those who have adopted a wild burro through the government's program, are afraid of getting kicked. Donkeys that have not been properly gentled will not readily allow their hooves to be touched. Many farriers will refuse to work on donkeys that are not manageable for fear of injury and the owners are left without any other resources. In 'cowboy' areas of our country one solution that is used all too often is to rope the donkeys legs and pull the animal to the ground. This method actually compounds the donkey's fear of trimming and results is an even wilder and more untrusting animal. If no help can be found, readily and at an affordable price, the donkey's hooves are left to grow uncorrected. Many times this leads to irreversible problems, lameness and even death.

Wild burros suffering from improper management and loss of habitat.

From as early as 1600 AD., donkeys have been released into the wilds of the Americas. During the early years of exploration, development and settlement of the New World, donkeys have been used by man and then released when their services were no longer needed. Because of the donkey's natural ability to adapt to dry, arid climates, they thrive in the deserts of the American South West . Donkeys, or burros as their non-domesticated cousins are referred to, continue to breed throughout their long lives and can therefore over-populate a region without proper management. Donkeys also have no natural predators and this contributes to over stress on the environment. In 1972 the Free Roaming Wild Horse and Burro Act was passed by the US Government to protect these wild animals on Public Lands. This was later limited to only those lands administered by the Bureau of Land Management. It is under the management of the BLM that some wild herds are managed but only as long as funding is available to actually count the burros in the protected regions. Otherwise there is no management only decimation.

On other lands managed by the US Fish and Wildlife Service, the

National Park Service and state agencies, burros are looked upon as feral and can be removed by lethal force. These agencies have no resources for the management of wild burros and usually are forced to take the least expensive option to eradicate the burro population. Another constant threat to the stability and well being of wild burros is the conflict between themselves and local farmers and cattlemen. Often times wild burros will find themselves grazing on a farmer's crops or competing with cattle for water on public lands. Wild burros have no common voice and find themselves at the mercy at the powerful lobbying groups that control so much of our government.

Melquiades

Melquiades and I have been together for many years and have had some great adventures together. Since he is a big part of the Texas Burro Rescue and the project to save the Big Bend Ranch Burros, I thought I would share his story and how he came to be part of our rescue.

His story is pretty typical of so many of the donkeys that come into our rescue. There were some people that had a donkey and they had been evicted from their mobile home. For whatever reason they left their donkey behind. County Animal Control had been called in but had no means to catch and transport a donkey. So, as we often do, we offered our services to help this donkey. Now this mobile home was in a trailer park literally in the middle of nowhere. It was obvious that all of the residents of this park were poor, very poor.

Two things struck me immediately when I saw this donkey: he was one of the tallest donkeys I had ever seen and he was emaciated.

He was standing in two feet of his own manure and there was nothing around for him to eat. There was, oddly enough, a little pink bucket of clean fresh water. The bucket seemed a little out of place in this drab, disgusting pen. On closer inspection I noticed it was a child's sand bucket, one that you could make sand castles with at the beach.

Amy and I were able to get this mammoth donkey into the trailer with surprisingly little trouble, he was ready to go. Anywhere was better than where he was. As we shook hands with the Animal Control Officer, I noticed a little girl standing a ways off holding a plastic grocery sack.

I smiled and waved to her and I noticed she was crying. Not wanting to scare her, I asked Amy to find out if she was OK. When Amy returned she said she couldn't understand the little girl because she only spoke Spanish. Now I'm no linguist, but I can speak enough Spanish to get by, so I walked over and greeted her with my best "Buenos tardes muchacha" to which she burst into tears and said, "El nombre de burro es Melquiades." Because of her sobs and nervousness it took me a few times of hearing it but finally I understood that she was telling me that the name of this donkey was Melquiades.

As I was talking with her, I noticed that the bag she was carrying contained the remnants of vegetable stalks and peelings that had obviously been cut for her family's dinner. She told me that every night after dinner she would bring the burro grande (big donkey) whatever food she could find. Her family was very poor but she had taken it upon herself to try and help this starving, abandoned donkey. The people who had owned Melquiades were "muy mal" (very bad) and did cruel things to him before they abandoned him. When they were not around she would sneak over and pet Melquiades. When the people left they didn't even leave his water trough, so she had given him her very own pink bucket.

I let her stand on the side of the trailer and say good bye to her friend and it was evident that Melquiades loved this little girl. She had been the one bright spot in his miserable life and he licked her hand as she reached in to pet him goodbye. After I helped her down from the side of the trailer she ran into the donkey's enclosure, dumped the water out of the pink bucket and handed it to me, "para Melquiades." I thanked her for the bucket and for being such a good friend to Melquiades and promised to take care of him for the rest of his life.

It has been a few years since I picked up Melquiades but I never forgot that little girl and her pink bucket. For someone who had so little, this little girl was willing to give all that she had. I still have that little pink bucket, it helps remind me of compassion, self sacrifice and the unconditional love that a little girl had for a big donkey that no one loved.

Over the years, Melquiades became a very loyal friend. Once he had put some weight on, he followed me around like a puppy. It wasn't long before I got in the habit of putting his pack saddle on and letting him carry my tools as I worked around the ranch each day. Now that I am going to be spending so much time luring the wild burros into our traps on the Big Bend Ranch, I am sure Melquiades and I will have many new adventures to share with you.

The Burroman
Mark Meyers & Melquiades the mammoth burro

What's In A Word?

Many people misunderstand the terminology associated with the donkey. The word 'donkey' is derived from the Old English word 'dun' meaning gray and 'ky' meaning small. The word donkey has been around for hundreds of years and has become a term used to describe all members of the ass family. Most donkeys bear a cross on their back and some have zebra type stripes on their legs.

The word 'burro' originates from the Latin word for "little horse". In the United States, we use the terms to differentiate between the domesticated 'donkey' and wild free-ranging 'burro'. Therefore, a burro is wild and a donkey is domesticated. As they are from the same stock, there are no physical differences between the two. Wild burros in an area will often share a common look due to the herd's small initial gene pool.

A mule is an entirely different animal. A mule is a hybrid resulting from the mating of a jack, or male donkey, to a mare, a female horse. With rare exception, mules are sterile and cannot reproduce. A mule possesses the size, strength and work ethic of a horse while having the intelligence, sure footedness and sympathies of a donkey. Hinnies are a cross between a stallion, a male horse, and a jennet, a female donkey and are less common than mules.

Donkeys are measured in inches as opposed to "hands" whch is used for horses. Donkeys are classified into three groups based on height which is measured to the withers (shoulders). Because organizations tend to define the categories differently, there is no universal standard.

    Miniature   35" or less
    Standard   36" to 55"
    Mammoth   56" or above

Donkeys come in many color variations including:
White-Pink-Light Gray-Dark Gray-Brown-Red-Black and Spotted

Chester

When Chester came to us from an auction, he was caked in red mud. It was evident that he not only had been physically beaten, but mentally beaten as well. Chester seldom raised his head and showed little interest in interacting with other donkeys. Chester did not know what a carrot was and it took years before he would pick one up from the ground. Even then, Chester would never dream of taking one from a human hand.

When donkeys expect abuse, they will place themselves in a trance-like state known as a 'sully'. This is the donkey's way of removing themselves from the pain and terror. Billy, another jack that was purchased along with Chester and caked in the same red mud, also would sully when approached too quickly. Billy, however, was eventually able to overcome the abuse of his past and learn to love people. Chester never forgot the horrors of his past no matter how hard I tried, he was simply too traumatized.

Chester died from throat cancer on Thanksgiving a few years back. It seemed a sad irony because this donkey had so little to be thankful for in his pitiful life. I wish I could have given him a year of happiness for every year of misery he had experienced. Chester will always be a tragedy to me. He was one story that never had a happy ending. He never made friends, he was always terrified of people and in the entire time I knew him, he never seemed happy.

Bunny

At my twentieth high school reunion, I was standing around with a group of my old high school buddies. Eventually the conversation turned to our respective occupations: a doctor, a lawyer, a couple of engineers, a handful of contractors. Then someone asked me what I did. When I replied that I rescued donkeys, the group exploded with laughter. "You have to be joking! Why?"

When you work with donkeys, you come to expect this kind of response. You get the usual barrage of ass jokes and plenty of laughs all around. I understand their laughter. They don't know, they haven't seen and they never met Bunny.

Bunny was found in a junkyard. Her owners thought it would be a good idea to use a donkey as a weed eater. But, once Bunny had eaten all the weeds, the owners did not think she was important enough to be fed. With no more food, Bunny was forced to look for anything and everything that might be edible. Slowly starving to death, she began eating old wood that was covered with lead paint. When we rescued Bunny, she was already suffering from brain damage and liver failure.

Because we knew Bunny's time with us was short, my family was committed to staying with her until the end. Our greatest fear was that she would slip away alone and sad. Amy and I spent every available minute with Bunny, and when other responsibilities called us away, our kids would take over.

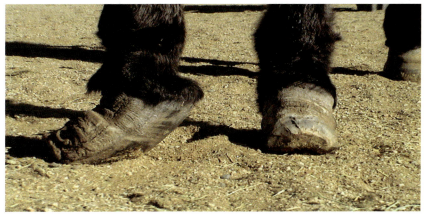

As the days progressed, Christmas drew near. We did not have any presents for the family yet, so when Amy and I went to town to do our shopping, the children stayed with Bunny. When we returned, we learned that our youngest son Jake had refused to leave Bunny's side, even for moment. As I joined him and sat down next to Bunny, my six-year-old child looked up at me and said, "Why do people get animals if they are not going to take care of them?" And with saying that, he burst into tears. At six years of age, this child had a deeper understanding of the suffering of animals and the responsibility that goes along with animal ownership than most adults. He understood 'why' we do what we do.

We lost Bunny on Christmas Eve. We can only hope that we brought some degree of comfort to her otherwise lonely and miserable life. And while Christmas in the traditional sense did not hold much magic, in a greater sense it was the best Christmas ever. It was the year that my family was able to share the gift of compassion and selflessness. I only wish more people could understand 'why'.

Picture taken by Jake Meyers on Bunny's last morning.

Diesel vs. My Conscious

I almost didn't go. The little town in North Texas was over 300 miles one way from my ranch in Miles, Texas. The policeman on the phone said that if we didn't want him, they might be able to get rid of him some other way. There was something in the indifferent tone in his voice that made me realize that I needed to go. Everyone knows how expensive fuel is and traveling 600 miles round trip, for one donkey, didn't make good financial sense. But if I stopped rescuing donkeys simply because of fuel cost, then maybe I'm in the wrong business.

I didn't have enough money in my Texas Burro Rescue Account to cover the cost of the fuel, so I withdrew some money out my personal savings. I hooked up the trailer and headed north with my two traveling companions, Larry and Bonny.

I can't tell you a lot about the rescue because it is still under criminal investigation. But I can tell you that I felt terrible guilt for even letting the thought cross my mind that I shouldn't come get this donkey. He was on old jack, very skinny. There wasn't much in his pasture to eat and I could even find places on the trees where he had tried to eat the bark. His hooves were long and he had a sad broken look in his eyes.

The policeman, I met at the property, offered to rope the donkey and help me drag him into the trailer, to which I promptly replied "Thanks, but no thanks". I walked slowly up to him and bent low so that he could see that I wasn't a threat. I talked to him for a while, telling him that everything was going to be 'OK'. And as I turned away from him to return to my truck to get a halter and rope, the old jack just followed me. As I walked into the trailer, he stepped right in behind me.

The policeman was amazed. "Well I guess you speak pretty good burro," he said with a laugh.

"Burros I can understand, people that treat animals like this, I don't understand at all." I replied.

As we finished the paperwork, a car drove by and rolled down a window. "Too bad you didn't come out here a month ago" a woman said, "you could have taken both of them. I think the other one is still over in the trees."

And sure enough, on closer inspection, I found the remains of a second donkey. It was hard to tell, but it had probably died from malnutrition. The really sad part was that the surviving donkey had to live with the sight of his friend's decaying body. Another rush of guilt washed over me for putting the cost of fuel over the well being of the animals that I have pledged to save. I named the old boy Diesel, as a reminder of the mistake I almost made.

I can run at speeds over 30 mph...

I can survive in the harshest climates...

I will not run from danger, but will confront it...

I can live four days without water and eat the barest desert scrub...

If you treat me kindly, I will be your most faithful friend...

What is so funny about being a jackass?
Peaceful Valley Donkey Rescue   www.donkeyrescue.org

Hey You...JACKASS!

At our Tehachapi Ranch, we host thousands of school age children in our Compassionate Learning Center field trip program. My favorite ages for these trips is the fourth graders. There is something about this age that is fun. They are old enough to understand the concepts that you are teaching them, yet they are not at that 'too cool' stage.

During the field trips, my job is to talk about donkeys. Trying to fill 30 minutes just on donkeys can be quite a challenge. I usually tell a few stories, explain the terminology surrounding donkeys and explain what a Jackass is. Just saying the word Jackass makes the kids laugh, and laugh, and laugh. But then I explain to them what a Jackass is, and more importantly what it can do. Usually by the end of my time, no one thinks that Jackass is that funny anymore.

Almost every culture has something in common: they all use 'jackass' as a derogatory slur. The term conjures visions of stupidity, stubbornness and lack of common sense. Bugs Bunny always turned into a donkey when he did something stupid. When Pinocchio and the other boys were greedy and lustful, they all became donkeys. These are examples of what is ingrained in our social psyche. We do not know where we learned that donkeys are stubborn and stupid, we simply came to accept it as fact.

We asked two questions in a shopping center poll:

Question #1: Can you name 3 characteristics of a donkey?
Top three answers: Stubborn, Stupid and Dangerous

Question #2: Have you ever personally met, touched or seen a donkey?
Not one person polled said yes

With such an ingrained yet undeserved reputation, it is no wonder American donkeys are widely abused and neglected. If I were to refer to another man as a jackass, it would be considered mean, antagonistic, and even threatening. But what is a jackass? A jackass is simply a male donkey, usually non-castrated. They can weigh more than 800 pounds. They are one of the fastest mammals on the planet and can endure four days in a scorching desert without water. They can kill most predators and are extremely intelligent. They have been known to risk themselves to protect loved ones and they can be the most loyal friends you will ever find.

So now, if I were to call you a jackass, would you still be offended?

Jobe

This story of Jobe has been amended to include the fight that occurred between Jobe and I. It was originally omitted because many people thought that it sent the wrong message about rescue. I have put it back in because I feel that it is important to note that "time outs" do not work in the animal world and sometimes aggression must be met with aggression. I do not beat animals and I have never intentionally hurt an animal, but in a fight between a 250 pound man and a 600 pound donkey, the odds are with the donkey. Well.. unless he's fighting me.

The Peaceful Valley Donkey Rescue received a call from a caregiver to an elderly man. The man, it was explained, was very old and would forget to feed his donkey. The caregiver was only scheduled to visit the man two days a week and was unable to ensure the donkey was fed as needed. The caregiver contacted the elderly man's son, who, through his power of attorney, was able to transfer ownership of the donkey to us.

When we arrived to pick up the donkey, the summer sun was beating down in triple digits. My first impression of him was one of grief. He was very thin and lethargic. He was cramped in a very small pen and his hooves were overgrown due to neglect. Upon examination, the donkey proved to be eighteen years old and a whole jack. Because of his weakened condition, he was unable to muster much of a fight and was easily loaded into our trailer.

As is our habit, we discussed a name on the long ride home. A number of suggestions were made and rejected until I came up with the name Job—the biblical figure with infinite patience. (The spelling was later changed to Jobe because I got tired of people mispronouncing it.) This donkey must have had an enormous amount of patience to wait all of those long years in a small pen on the brink of starvation to finally be rescued.

Upon arrival at the Rescue, Jobe was given a thorough medical examination. He was brought up to date on his vaccinations and worming and his overgrown hooves were corrected. We discussed what should be done about gelding. Because of his age, malnourished condition and the tendency of donkeys to be heavy bleeders, we decided that Jobe would not be gelded right away.

As his health improved, Jobe was placed in a bachelor group of other male donkeys. The result was chaos. Jobe attacked the entire herd simultaneously. If any of the other donkeys did not run from his attack, he would launch into the most brutal assault that we had ever witnessed, his teeth and hooves flashing in fury. I immediately separated Jobe from the herd, but the damage was done. Jobe would not relax. He would bray challenges across the field to the other males and try desperately to break out of his pen.

As the head trainer for the Rescue, it was my responsibility to work with Jobe on a daily basis. With his newfound aggression, however, training sessions were more like acts of self-defense. Jobe would constantly charge me, trying to bite. If this failed, he would rear up on his hind legs and flail his hooves at my head. This fighting continued daily until one night, Jobe caught the scent of a jenny in season. He succeeded in tearing down two gates in an attempt to reach her.

Amy heard the commotion and ran outside in time to see Jobe in the arena with many of the other donkeys. Since I was not home, it was up to her to separate them. By the time she managed to get most of the donkeys secured, Jobe focused his aggression on her. Sensing the danger, Amy ran to the safety of the house with Jobe only inches behind her. He kept a close watch on the front door and would not allow Amy to venture outside again. When I returned, Jobe was captured and placed in an even more secure pen with heavy chains protecting the gates.

It was decided that Jobe had to be gelded right away. He was not only a danger to people and other donkeys, but he had no quality of life in his current condition. Dr. John, was called to perform the procedure. To reduce bleeding, great care was taken to crimp the vessels and tie them off, a process known as ligation. Because of Dr. Roueche's expertise, Jobe recovered quickly from the procedure.

Jobe's aggressive tendencies had not been reduced as we had hoped. One afternoon, he jumped his fence and entered a pasture with Rawhide. Now Rawhide is a lover and not a fighter and was taking a horrible beating. When I heard the commotion I immediately jumped into the fight, trying top break them apart. In his rage, Jobe turned on me. He

reared on his hind legs and tried to come down on my shoulders, in order to drive me to the ground where I would be easy pickings. I was able to sidestep the flailing hooves and punched him several times as he came down.

Next, Jobe tried to come in with his teeth, again I was able to block his move and got a square punch to his snout. Jobe backed up for a minute and I seized the opportunity to get him in a head lock. Jobe reared and ran, he tried to drag me along a fence and when that didn't work he knelt down to his front knees trying to take me off balance. Finally, after what seemed like an eternity, Jobe relaxed in my arms. I felt all of the aggression and pent up energy subside. Slowly I released my hold, and Jobe just stood there motionless.

From that day forward, Jobe was a new donkey. He stopped fighting unless provoked and he was able to become a member of the herd. Jobe was the first to greet me when I came into the paddock, and would challenge any other donkeys that he felt we getting too close to me. He became so protective of me that one day I was leading a donkey from our medical facilities through the barn yard when the donkey dashed away from me and mounted a crippled jennet. I was desperately trying to get the large jack off of the jennet when a brown blur swept passed me.

Jobe had seen the altercation, jumped two fences and hit the other jack like a linebacker. He continued to beat up on the larger opponent until I walked to him and said his name. He immediately stopped and took a step back, obviously proud of himself for his accomplishment.

Jobe is a busy donkey these days. He is a part of our field trip program and allows the children to pet and brush him. He also is one of my pack team members, his main job is to patrol the camp each night and ensure that no wild jacks molest the other donkeys in camp.

Left: Rawhide

Center: Acclaimed Filmmaker Pella Erickson

Right: Jobe

My Dear Sweet Clara

Clara was purchased at an auction along with two other donkeys. When she arrived at the Rescue, it was evident that Clara was special. She was short in stature, only 38" at the withers, but had a huge belly. Everyone thought that Clara was pregnant. Clara, before coming to us, had been bred over and over again, once she had been used up, she was discarded. Her huge belly was a result of the many pregnancies and improper diet.

Clara had a warmth and love that made her everyone's favorite. She went on many trips to schools, churches and anywhere people needed to know just how sweet a donkey could be. Clara had a mischievous way of 'goosing' people who ignored her and her short height made her an expert at it. On more than one occasion, I would be giving a tour to a group of people and Clara would goose one of them making them scream from surprise. I don't know how many donations we lost because of her.

We lost Clara to a stroke that left her paralyzed and eventually took her life. During her last days, we desperately tried every treatment known to veterinary medicine. We even tried acupuncture, but nothing was going to bring my Clara back. Not a day goes by that I do not think of Clara with both a laugh and a tear. I have so many fond memories of my time with Clara, she will always be remembered as one of the best.

Josh, Jake & Clara
June 2002

Rawhide

Late one hot summer afternoon, the Peaceful Valley Donkey Rescue received a phone call from a local horse trader. This particular horse trader had come across a donkey at auction with severe scarring on his legs, ears and nose. Many horse traders look upon animals as a commodity and nothing more. This donkey, however, affected this man in such a way that he felt he needed to do something for it.

Having no real experience with donkeys, the trader phoned the Peaceful Valley Donkey Rescue. We have a standing offer to pick up abused and neglected donkeys anywhere, anytime. After receiving the call, Amy and I grabbed the keys to the truck, hitched up the trailer and began our journey to pick up this donkey.

When we arrived at the horse trader's ranch, our first impression of the donkey was one of sadness. This donkey looked defeated. His eyes were glazed, his head hung to the ground and his ears never moved. It was apparent from the brief inspection that this unfortunate animal was the victim of roping. His rear legs were scarred from rope burns, his ears were notched and his nose was cut.

During the ride home, Amy and I discussed a name for this new addition to the Rescue. We had many donkeys named for famous people: Waylon and Willie, Martin and Lewis, Doc and Wyatt, Patsy (Cline) and even a Marilyn (Monroe). It was felt that this donkey needed an important

Me & Rawhide on the top of the Panamint Mountains overlooking Death Valley.

name. A name that would remind people of his past while at the same time allowing him to start anew. The name Rawhide seemed to fit so well that no other suggestion even came close.

Upon arrival at the Rescue, Rawhide instantly sprang to life at the sounds of braying from the many other residents. He began to pace in his pen and answer the challenges of the other males. With his newfound vigor, Rawhide began to show resentment of human presence in his pen. He would retreat to a far corner and stand with his rear facing the intruder, not allowing anyone to touch him or even come close to him.

Amy and I took turns working with Rawhide in an effort to regain his trust in people. Many hours were spent sitting quietly in his pen letting him get used to the presence of people once again. After several weeks of this non-intrusive 'contact', Rawhide began showing signs of curiosity. He would walk to within 10 feet and study us completely. This distance slowly receded over time until Rawhide would stand almost touching the person sitting in the pen. The impulse to reach out to Rawhide had to be suppressed since it was felt that he needed to be allowed to make first contact. This would help to build his confidence and give him control over the situation.

After a time, Rawhide initiated contact. First with a quick sniff and a brush of his whiskers and later with a longer more inquisitive touch of his muzzle. At this point, it was evident that Rawhide was ready to be touched again. I started the very next session by slowly walking up to Rawhide. I turned slightly sideways and stooped over to appear smaller. I then reached out and touched Rawhide's shoulder. Rawhide tensed for a moment, then relaxed with a sigh. The standoff was over. Rawhide was on his way to recovery.

Things progressed quickly for Rawhide after that day. He would allow us to brush him, treat the wounds on his body and pet him all over. He also showed that he trusted our children when they would clean pens or feed. Rawhide was quickly regaining his self-confidence and his trust in people.

After his quarantine period was over, Rawhide was placed in a pen with other donkeys in a social group. It was apparent that Rawhide didn't have social skills since he kept attacking other male donkeys in the herd. Often, I would have to race to Rawhide's rescue when another donkey would hurt him as a result of his initiating a fight. Each time that I would intervene on his behalf, Rawhide would stand behind me with his head resting on the small of my back.

With his outgoing personality, Rawhide quickly became the hit of the Rescue. When people toured the grounds and met the many donkeys, Rawhide would follow the group. He wanted attention. He would stand quietly beside them, hoping for a kind word or a scratch on the ears. Although many offers were made to adopt him, we had simply grown too attached to Rawhide to ever see him leave our care.

    Part of Rawhide's continuing therapy included many walks in the desert with me. Because of his newfound trust and affection, Rawhide followed me everywhere. As the training progressed, Rawhide learned to carry packs on an old-fashioned sawbuck packsaddle. It wasn't long until Rawhide and I were taking overnight trips together all over the state.

    On one of these pack trips, we were traveling along an old dusty road when we happened upon a gated house. Behind the fence were four large dogs that barked at our approach. Not used to seeing people or donkeys walking near their territory, the dogs raised quite a ruckus. After passing the house, I was startled as Rawhide's body language suddenly changed. He had noticed something and grown tense. I followed his eyes and ears just in time to see a pair of large black dogs stalking us from the brush.

    Obviously responding to the barking of the fenced dogs at the house, the stalkers closed in on us growling and snarling. At a distance of twenty feet, they separated and began to circle. Rawhide, sensing the danger, kept a wary eye on the two dogs. Not wanting Rawhide to be attacked while tied, I took off his lead rope. Now free, Rawhide began circling me in an effort to protect me from the dogs. When one of the stalkers would approach, Rawhide would charge out, keeping it at bay. Finally, when Rawhide was between both dogs and me, he made his move. He rushed at them at full speed, ears pinned and teeth bared.

Suddenly losing their confidence, both dogs quickly took flight. Rawhide, at full speed, was hot on their trail. He stomped one dog killing it instantly. Then he quickly disappeared from view, leaving me to worry about my friend. Not wanting to leave the spot where Rawhide might return, I waited for him. After twenty minutes with no sign of my friend, I set out to track Rawhide and discover his whereabouts. As I followed the trail, I grew more and more nervous. What if Rawhide was hurt? What if the remaining dog turned the tables on him? What if Rawhide found his way to a road and was hit by a car? My tensions grew with each passing minute until desperation began to tie my stomach in knots.

And then, as suddenly as he had disappeared, Rawhide returned. Trotting over a dune with his head held high, Rawhide greeted me with a look that simply said, 'Friends'.

Rawhide's story has been made into a television show that is still shown internationally.

```
Old Roy
```

Now that the Texas Burro Rescue is open for business, the burros are lining up, waiting to get in. One of the newest arrivals is an old white burro with a bad hip. He was roped by a contract wrangler on the Federal Park and brought to the USDA facility near Ojinaga, Mexico. Burros have no financial value along the Rio Grande so TBR gets all that come along, as long as we pay the holding fee of $5.00 per day.

This particular old burro made me smile from the second I saw him. It was not his disability or his poor body weight, it was his eyes. Even in his pitiful state, he still had the eye of a confident old man. He was not the least bit impressed with me and when I pressured him too close he even offered a kick. Bad leg not withstanding, he almost got me!

As he probably came from Mexico and since my book has not yet been published in Spanish, I quickly realized that he had no idea who I was. So for the next hour he tried to kick me and I tried to remember all of the swear words I knew in Spanish. Fortunately my profanity won the day, as it usually does, and he reluctantly walked into the trailer.

After I got him back the Miles' Ranch, I placed him in a separate pen away from the other burro residents. I was worried about his weight and overall condition and didn't want to add any stress by having him compete with the younger jacks.

In an attempt to fatten him up a little, I put him on a diet of hay and Equine Senior. (For those who do not regularly buy feed, Equine Senior is an expensive and apparently very tasty feed for older equines). A diet that he not only loved, but grew hostile if he thought I was running a little late in giving it to him. Since his time in my care, he is putting on

weight and seems to be in good health.

    A few days after his arrival I was sitting on the top rail of his pen. He was braying at me as loud as he could when I realized how funny the whole situation was. Here I was living in Texas away from my family and catering to a crippled burro. One who the slaughter buyers wouldn't even turn into dogfood, and I was not only feeding, doctoring and pampering him, but I was getting kicked by him at every turn. So because of my undying devotion to animals that don't appreciate me, I named him Old Roy for the dog food that he will never become.

An Ode To Wyatt:
A Grumpy Old Fart

Wyatt came to us through a livestock auction in the early days. We were still a fledging donkey rescue when Amy picked him up. I was away on a pack trip at the time and when I returned home there was Wyatt and another donkey that Amy had named Doc. Wyatt was clearly the older of the pair and he had the scars of abuse all over him.

From early on, he made it perfectly clear that he was not interested in being people friendly. His actions and scars spoke for themselves' He had been mistreated and he was not going to forgive or forget. Wyatt did not consider himself a victim, he had too much pride.

Wyatt liked our 40+ year old Grandma instantly and they became inseparable. Perhaps it was her charm and grace, but I think it was the equine senior feed that she received each night. Either way, Wyatt had found a friend in Grandma.

Wyatt always made the rules when it came to his dealings with people. There was never an appropriate time for a scratch or even a touch. Worming, vaccines and hoof work were a nightmare. No matter how long Wyatt was with us, he never accepted humans. We were always having to catch him, then sedate him, then work on him. Wyatt had too much dignity, and was too grumpy to go easy.

After the move to Tehachapi, Wyatt became a permanent member of our Active Senior Center. Each morning and night he received his beloved ration of senior feed. He was in a low stress environment and had

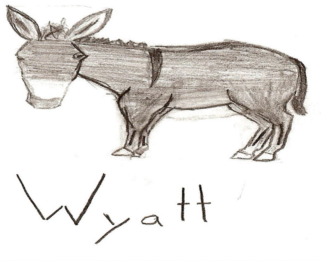

A sketch by a little girl named Chloe. She helped sponsor Wyatt with her own money, because she didn't think anybody else would love him.

plenty of company, donkey company, the only kind he liked.

We found Wyatt dead the other day. He had a heart attack and literally dropped dead in his tracks. No pain, no suffering, just dead. The staff reacted as they do with all death. Grief, remorse and even guilt. What should they have done different? What could we have done to save him? But to them, Wyatt was just another unfriendly donkey. They really didn't know him.

Amy and I had a different reaction. It was one of reverence. We knew Wyatt. With us, Wyatt was the embodiment of why we rescue donkeys. I think people look at animal rescue through very rosy glasses. They think of an animal, once rescued, of being loving, friendly and most importantly, appreciative to the rescuers. This is usually not the case and Wyatt was the poster child!

As I knelt beside his body, I reflected back over our many years together. I thought of all the times that I chased him around the pen. The many occasions when he would deal me a swift kick and the one time he managed to bite me on the arm. These memories were not angry ones, but rather joyful ones. If Amy had never saved him all those years ago, Wyatt would never have had the opportunity to act like the cantankerous old fart that he was. He would also not have had the chance to die with dignity. Wyatt was always a worthy adversary, and I for one miss him greatly.

Snoopy's Spot

Every morning I see him standing in the same spot as I open the gate to the sanctuary. A lone, dark shape distinguished from the others only by his broken and bent ear. Snoopy, a name I gave him as he entered the trap that was set up in a remote Nevada Desert a few years ago, has not forgotten his previous life. His territory is no longer an expanse of desert wilderness shadowed by majestic peaks, but is now just a little spot of ground inside of Paddock 1. From the time of his arrival here in Tehachapi, this has been his spot. He stands there and stares south. I would trade what little I have to be able to listen to his thoughts.

Snoopy was one of many wild burros that were "too many" for the government's liking. Reduction, elimination, removal for ecological stability, name the euphemism and it still boils down to burros being removed from the wild. I have studied the issues, read the reports and been personally involved in the management of wild burro herds. Nothing, in all of my studies or my experiences, has ever taken away the guilt I feel when I look into the eyes of a burro like Snoopy. Snoopy is a wild burro, not a politician, or a cattleman, or a hunter, or a "special interest" group, and he will spend the rest of his life trying to understand why he is no longer in his beloved desert.

Within days of his capture, Snoopy was a fairly friendly guy. He

was the only male captured in this particular group and spent his quarantine time alone away from the jennets that had come in with him. He was never aggressive and never snorted at my approach as so many of the new arrival jacks often do. Snoopy was quiet and he and I spent a great deal of time talking and getting to know one another. The truth be told, I did most of the talking. Snoopy wasn't much of a talker. These strong silent types often don't like to share their feelings and Snoopy was no exception. After his castration and all through his recovery our friendship grew. He didn't like strangers and would avoid me if anyone else was around. Some of the staff even thought that I was joking when I would talk of our friendship, after all, they had never seen it.

Snoopy is a member of our 'B' herd. 'B' means nothing more here than 'Not A'. The 'A' herd gets most of the attention from the guests, field trip children and training staff. The 'A' herd is our adoptable group and therefore are the safest ones to be around. The 'B's' are a large herd and have their own social order. Many of the B herd have come from abusive or neglected backgrounds. They are here to heal emotionally. In this setting they can become a donkey again and forget some of the horrors of their past. Others, like Snoopy, are captured wild burros trying to adjust to a domestic life. Many do. They adjust, accept people, and find a new adoptive home with a loving family, but not all.

Snoopy stands his post, on his spot, every minute of every day. When the feed wagon comes by, Snoopy is the last one to leave the field and find a place to eat. As soon as he has finished his meal and satisfied his thirst, he returns to his spot and resumes his southward stare. I try my best to provide everything that the donkeys within my care need. The lengths I go to and the things I have done are the subject of many jokes by my friends and family. The herd assignments, the paddock rotations, the types and placements of shelters, are all thought and rethought and then anguished over. But I can't help but think I have missed something when it comes to Snoopy.

Why that spot? Why hasn't he found a friend or a group of buddies? Why does he always stare south? I stood out there, on his spot, and stared South with him for awhile just the other day. It was a rare treat. These days I spend more time on airplanes then in paddocks. Instead of talking with donkeys, I am usually building new ranches or talking to donors. I kind of miss the simpler times. The times when my business covered the Rescue's expenses and I could spend as much time as I wanted with my beloved donkeys. But now with ever growing hay costs, increasing medical expenses and our plan to affect the plight of donkeys on a national level, I am the only one who can plead the donkey's case and so more and more of my time is spent on the road.

During our brief visit on his spot, I asked him if he was thinking of his desert home. I inquired if he had friends there that he missed. I tried to explain politics and why some burros were rounded up and others where shot. But mostly, I did the talking and he just stood there and stared south.

Baby

We received a call from donkey owners who were going on vacation for a month. They wanted us to catch, provide veterinary care and train their donkey while they were gone. We found out that this family had owned Baby since she was just a few months old, hence the name Baby, but had never spent any time with her. They had never even touched her! This 12-year-old jenny had never been petted, brushed and especially caught.

It was a bit of a challenge to get Baby away from the two horses. Every time we tried to cut the horses, Baby followed them as if she was glued to them. After nearly an hour, we finally managed to get this wild and very scared donkey into the trailer and head for the ranch.

After being with us for just two weeks, Baby turned into one of the sweetest donkeys we have ever known. She was the first to greet us at the gate and she walked loyally alongside anyone who ventured into her paddock. She loved to be brushed and would walk around with the brush in her mouth hoping to coax someone into using it on her.

When the owners returned, that called us and said that we could bring Baby back whenever we wanted. I asked them to come to the Rescue and spend time getting to know Baby. This way, when she returned home, they would have already laid the groundwork for their new relationship and everyone would be much happier. The owners decided that they did not want to go to that much trouble and signed her over to us. Baby has gone from a lonely donkey in a field to a loving donkey with a family.

Peggy

An elderly couple was moving from their ranch into a retirement home and could no longer keep their donkey. They loved this donkey dearly and had cared for her for more than 20 years. In their effort to ensure a good home, they called the Rescue several times, looked over our website, read our policies and came out for a tour of the facility and to meet the staff.

During the tour of the donkey area, the man stated that his donkey had a fat neck, unlike the donkeys at the Rescue. He said that it had gotten larger over time until it finally flopped over to one side. I explained that donkeys are desert animals and they cannot metabolize rich foods. As a result, fat is stored in various places, the neck being one of the most obvious. This loving couple began to weep after realizing they were responsible for their beloved donkey's condition. They decided to place her in the care of the Rescue.

Peggy was in her early twenties, pink in color and with fat deposits on her neck and on her sides. She also has more love and personality than can be described. Like many older jennets, Peggy has a motherly nature. She likes to stand over me and lick my head, protecting me from other donkeys. She is good-natured, has a deep love of all people, and is extremely intelligent.

Peggy makes it a point to walk with every tour group. She stays very close so that she can love on them as only a donkey can. Still, group after group, adoption after adoption, no one has ever wanted Peggy. No one has ever come forward and said that it is because of her appearance. Instead, they find other ways of not choosing her. Sadly, they have missed out on a wonderful opportunity to know true love.

Peggy remains at the Rescue to this day. In many ways, I am glad that no one has adopted her. I hate to think of life without her motherly gaze and her loving kisses

Poncho and Lefty

They sneak across the border, usually at night. It is extremely dangerous and capture is always first on their mind. Looking up and down the Rio Grande, they scan for the presence of people. When the coast is clear, they make their move. Dashing across the shallow river and on toward what they hope is a better life.

But all too often, they get caught. And before I came along, they were usually killed. Poncho and Lefty were two burros that I was able to save.

What did you think I was talking about?

Burros in Mexico are treated even more cruelly than they are in the United States. Considered valueless, Mexican burros are used hard until they escape or die. Many of these burros are used along the border for smuggling. Packed with drugs, they are driven back and forth across the river. When released or escaped from their owners, they will return to the Texas side because the grazing is better.

These domestic burros are typically caught because they do not possess the instincts of their wilder cousins. Once caught, they have to be quarantined and blood tests have to be done to ensure that they have not brought any viruses or parasites into the United States. Once they are considered to be a non-threat to American Agriculture, the government doesn't know what to do with them. Because they hold no real value, the Government cannot sell them and would often times use euthanasia as a means of disposal. I have remedied this problem by agreeing to pay the boarding fees and handle all of the transportation costs.

Poncho and Lefty show the signs of abusive work. Saddle sores so bad that it was obvious that they were loaded again and again even though their backs were a bloody mess. Scars around their ankles, just above the hoof, where they had been hobbled with wire as a means to keep them still. Both of them are extremely head shy and that is always an indictor of being struck.

Lefty is having trouble keeping weight on and is now on a special diet. He is not very friendly but allows me to scratch him as long as I keep bringing him the good feed. Poncho is better with his people skills. He still gets jumpy if I move too quickly, but he doesn't mind me brushing him.

Generally speaking, animals in the Mexican culture are not treated well. Mexican Rodeos are one of the most cruel and inhumane spectacles ever witnessed. This treatment of animals, and the culture behind it, comes from their Spanish roots. In Spain, there are many festivals and events that center around the abuse and even torture of animals. Bull fighting, when viewed for what it is, is an extremely brutal sport. In another annual event, a donkey is lead along a village street as all of the villagers pile onto its back until the donkey is finally crushed to death.

In Mexico, a very common site is the 'Mexican Zebra'. A donkey painted nose to tail, to look like a zebra. The donkey is then placed in front of a sombrero stand and usually tied there with wire and unable to move. Tourists enjoy getting their pictures taken with the Mexican Zebra and therefore the practice continues.

Photo by Donna Hardy

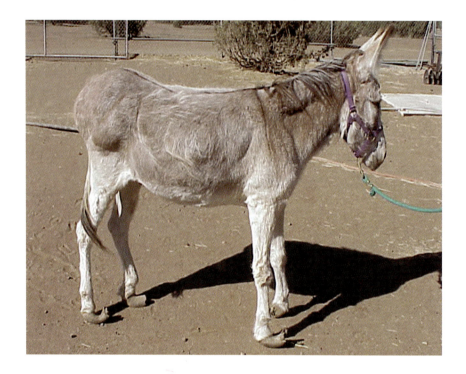

Genie

    Genie came from a central California cattle ranch where she was never given a hoof trim. The cattle on the ranch were especially well cared for, but after all, they had value. We were called in after a hay truck backed over Genie's owner. Ending his life and Genie's neglect. All four of Genie's hooves were horribly overgrown, each measuring thirteen inches. Our staff of experts worked tirelessly on Genie providing special trims, shoes, surgeries, casts and supports. No expense was spared in trying to rehabilitate this poor donkey.

    After a full year of treatments, I made the decision to end Genie's suffering. The damage was too severe and all we were doing was prolonging her pain. Despite having to endure so much, as we desperately tried to overcome her neglect, Genie was amazingly gentle and loving through it all. I have no doubt that she knew, at long last, that she was truly loved. It is a bitter thought when you realize that all of this could have been prevented by a $25.00 hoof trim.

Kenny

It started out as a rumor,
"Did you hear about the old man that got attacked by a donkey? It put him in the hospital."

And sure enough, a few hours later, Amy and I were on our way to go pick up the donkey. By the time we arrived, the owners had the little jack corralled. He was pacing and snorting and kept charging through the bars of the stall. Ignoring the protests of the owners, I jumped into the stall, got the donkey in a head lock and Amy was able to get a halter on him. Once Amy was clear, I grabbed the halter tightly and drug the little fellow into the trailer and slammed the door.

Once everyone was settled, we were told the whole story. Kenny, as he would be named by our ranch hands later, was born at this ranch. A well meaning but ill-informed woman mistook a mother's discipline for abuse and took the foal away. Kenny was bottle fed in a house and raised like one of the human children. As he got bigger, he was moved to the backyard and then recently to the pasture. Kenny was around three years old when they moved him into the pasture and the sight and smell of other donkeys nearby kicked his sexual maturity into high gear. The man, along with his grandchild, entered the pasture to pet Kenny as they had done many times when he lived in the backyard. That proved to be almost fatal.

A three year old donkey, while not full grown, is very danger-

ous. Kenny was made even more dangerous because he had no respect for other donkeys or for humans. Because he was denied the opportunity to grow up as a donkey, learning hierarchy and discipline as a donkey should, he did not know his boundaries. When he was given a new area near other donkeys, his territorial instincts kicked in. The man was in the wrong place at the wrong time. Fortunately he was able to recover from his injuries.

Once we had Kenny back at the ranch, we knew we would have to proceed carefully. He was extremely dangerous. He would attack anyone that came near his pen, forcing us to use caution tape and orange rubber cones to keep people a safe distance away. During tours, he would pace his pen and bray, constantly challenging anyone who would listen. Kenny did not differentiate between donkey or human. In his opinion both needed to be dominated.

Kenny's castration went well and he recovered quickly. The next phase was to get him to learn his place within a herd setting. The only logical setting was in the 'Knucklehead Pen'. The Knuckleheads are a group of misfits that do not fit in anywhere else. Melquiades and Ritchie are in there because they have a tendency of playing too rough and tearing down fences in the process. Stubbs is in there because he has an undescended testicle and cannot be allowed around jennets. All of the pony mules are in there because they don't get along with anyone else. Everyone in the Knucklehead herd is tough and more than confident in there position. A perfect setting for our young Kenny.

Kenny, true to form, went after the biggest donkey in the herd right away. This proved to be his undoing as Melquiades has never lost a fight. Mel quickly bit Kenny on the neck and then dropped all of is weight on Kenny's back forcing him to the ground. After a few minutes of holding him there, Mel released Kenny and Kenny staggered away. Next Kenny went after Ritchie, but fared no better. One by one, Kenny tried desperately to beat at least one member of the herd, but to no avail.

Over the next two weeks Kenny was the last to eat, the last to drink and the last to be allowed in the shelter. He was the low man on the totem pole and he finally realized just how tough he wasn't. It was a lesson he should have learned as a foal, but he definitely knew it now.

The next step was to make Kenny respect people. This is my job. Kenny would rush up on me as soon as I would enter his pen. My reaction was always the same, face him with both arms raised and quickly smack him on the nose. It only took a few times before he pulled up short. His training continued until he showed me the respect he should. Next we had to introduce other people. Just because he respected me did not mean he would automatically respect others, especially if the others were smaller than he was. The staff started working with him in the same manner as me until Kenny found his place among humans. He was now a donkey and a pretty good one at that.

Had Kenny's owners not removed him from his mother, all of this could have been avoided. People often misread the actions of animals and this instance could have been a lot worse. Kenny is now in Texas with me and is one of the friendliest and well behaved of the lot. I expect someone will adopt him very soon.

Part 2
MY RESCUE

I am very proud of the accomplishments that the Rescue has made. Like most rescues, Peaceful Valley started out very small, focusing on the animals within our community. As our reputation grew, so did the range of our travels. We were called into more and more rescue situations until we had to build more facilities to adequately handle the work.

A great deal of our success can be attributed to the fact that we never followed the same path as other rescues. We stayed our own course and did things our way. While we may have re-invented the wheel a few times, at the end of the day, we have created something unique.

This section will provide you with the concepts that the rescue was built upon as well as the facilities that we now have. Our mission to improve the Plight of the American Donkey is now well in sight.

The Problem With Hope

A successful animal rescue is visualized, built and maintained on three important principles:
1. Unfailing compassion
2. Limitless dedication
3. Keen Business Sense

Most rescues are created and managed by people with the best intentions. Unfortunately, best intentions without proper business skills are a disaster waiting to happen. What many people fail to realize is that rescue is an enormous undertaking and no matter how much you accomplish, there is always more left to do. One pitfall is for a rescue to take on more than it can handle.

In my career as an animal rescuer, I have witnessed some of the worst cases of abuse and neglect imaginable. It never ceases to amaze me how badly people can behave. Even 'good' people can justify very bad things. At times, it seems that almost no one is completely innocent.

Curiously enough, the worst abuse imaginable is not found in the auctions or the slaughter houses but in a place many people would never imagine. The worst cruelty that I have seen, is in some of our country's animal rescues.

In my opinion, the worst possible thing that you can do, to a human or an animal, is to give hope. Anyone or anything will eventually give into the despair of their existence and simply trudge through life waiting for it to be over. But to give hope only to snatch it away, is a fate far more cruel.

Peaceful Valley has seen this type of abuse on a first hand basis many times over. Animals rescued from abuse or neglect by a well intentioned rescue. But due to poor business management, financial hardship or just plain loss of interest, the animals are left to their own misery once again. We have seen overgrown hooves, parasite infestations, malnutrition and even signs of physical abuse on the animals that we confiscated from other rescues. In some areas, rescues have gained such unfavorable reputations, that county agencies will no longer deal with any rescue.

Peaceful Valley has avoided these pitfalls and has become not only the largest rescue of its kind, but the only one of its kind. We work directly with Federal, State, County and City agencies around the country. We have facilities all over the nation operated by people that have been trained by us. We are not a loose organization of people and places that share a common interest. We are in fact one professional organization able to respond in force to a situation anywhere in our country.

This section of the book was written to help you understand the structure and magnitude of our work.

The Solution

Public Perception

The vast majority of people in this country have never seen a real donkey. Peaceful Valley's Awareness and Outreach programs have taken donkeys into many places in order to introduce people to real, living donkeys. Schools, churches, Senior Centers, Swap Meets are a few examples of the places where people have had the opportunity to meet donkeys. Thousands of hearts have been changed in this hands-on way. Ingrained perceptions are changed as people see, for the first time, the gentleness, intelligence and compassion that donkeys have. School children, especially those that are of pre-high school age, have open minds and the ability to fully understand the positive attributes of donkeys and grow up with a non-prejudice opinion.

Abuse and neglect at the hands of ignorant owners

Education is the greatest weapon against ignorance. Many donkey owners simply do not have the resources at their disposal to learn proper methods of care, feeding and training. From the beginning, Peaceful Valley has fought the battle of ignorance at every turn. Even with eight television shows, thousands of hits on their websites each day, numerous radio interviews, countless newspaper and magazine articles and several thousand copies of my books sold, Peaceful Valley stills hears the excuse, "I didn't know".

A nation wide network of Peaceful Valley trained staff, volunteers working in their own communities, greater marketing coverage and a nationwide network of caring individuals is the only true solution to get the training and knowledge to the people and donkeys, that need it most. This knowledge had to be in an easy to read, easily available form. It had to be free of charge and contain the Peaceful Valley proven methods for care, feeding and gentling the American Donkey. The material was produced in the form of written materials, website pages, and video.

There is also a tremendous need for clinics or training sessions across the country. These clinics can be as small as a few people meeting in someone's back yard with a member of Peaceful Valley's trained staff. It could also be a huge event held in a rodeo arena or similar venue. Clinics of a wide variety must be provided to train not only donkey owners but also for our volunteer trainers, Satellite Adoption Center Operators and Peaceful Valley staff. The clinics have taught: hoof trimming, proper trailer loading, vaccine and de-worming techniques, gentling a wild burro, training to accept a halter and picking up all four hooves as well as teaching donkey owners patience.

Wild burros suffering from improper management and loss of habitat.
This area is one of the most difficult problems to solve. Currently, the responsibility of managing the wild burros on public lands falls directly under the Federal Government. As a Public Benefit Corporation, Peaceful Valley feels that it is our responsibility to assist the government by providing services and resources. A Public Benefit Corporation can react more quickly, provide many services at a lower cost and deal with problems both large and small.

Currently, the Bureau of Land Management has a management plan in place. While Peaceful Valley does not agree with some parts of this plan, we would prefer to continue our relationship with the BLM as it has existed for many years. Under our current arrangement, Peaceful Valley assists in BLM adoptions where the adopters who have problems with their wild burros can seek help from us. Once the animal is titled, usually after one year, the BLM can not take the animal back into its system. These animals are offered safe haven at Peaceful Valley. Under current legislation, any burro captured that is over ten years old must be sold and is not protected under the 1972 law. Peaceful Valley has worked closely with the supervisors in Washington D.C. to ensure that all of the burros that fell victim to this new law were safely placed with Peaceful Valley.

Most other agencies, both Federal and State, do not have a 'burro budget'. When faced with over population or other management issues these agencies turn to shooting. Peaceful Valley has stepped up our capture efforts to provide low and no cost capture assistance to these agencies. As populations grow and budget cuts deepen, Peaceful Valley is getting called upon more and more often.

Our Plan
The only real solution to all of the problems facing donkeys in the 21st Century is to provide a nationwide network of facilities and people. United under a common goal and organized under a single organization, the problems facing the American Donkey can be solved. While the task may seem daunting, it is actually quite feasible. In fact it is already under way. We simply need more resources to continue our growth as a national presence. By combining our corporate structure and leadership with a nationwide network of employees and volunteers, we can Improve The Plight of the American Donkey as well as continue to provide our high level of professional rescue services to every needy donkey in this country.

Our plan is based on the operation of three types of facilities. These facilities work together, in support of one and other, while performing their individual tasks. These facilities are:

Satellite Adoption Centers

Starting at the community level, Peaceful Valley Satellite Adoption Centers are the local contact points. These centers not only adopt out donkeys into pre-screened, qualified homes, but also act as a gateway for donkeys needing help to get into our system. The SAC's also distribute information, set up Donkey Awareness Booths at local events and play host to clinics on all types of donkey care. The SAC's are operated on private ranches and are staffed by volunteers. Peaceful Valley covers the expense of feed and medical care while the donkeys are at the SAC. The SAC operators act on behalf of Peaceful Valley and monitor all adopted donkeys in their area.

Corporate Rescue Ranch Facilities

In order to provide support to the SAC's, Peaceful Valley has three Corporate Ranch Facilities across the country. Our main Headquarters is in Tehachapi, California, our central division is in Miles, Texas and our eastern division is in Mineral, Virginia. These Rescue Ranch Facilities are staffed by paid Peaceful Valley employees. Each Rescue Ranch has holding paddocks, training arenas and minor medical facilities. Our main medical facilities remain in California. The management staff at each Rescue Ranch Facility has been trained in numerous disciplines including training, hoof trimming, minor medical treatment and trailering. From the Rescue Ranch Facilities, donkeys can be received in from the SAC's as well as move adoptable donkeys into communities where good homes are available.

Sanctuaries

To provide the best possible environment for our wild burros, Peaceful Valley is also constructing Sanctuaries. These Sanctuaries provide open spaces with natural grazing for the donkeys in our system that will never be adoptable. These burros, separated by sex to prevent breeding, are released onto sanctuary facilities and left to themselves. They are rounded up twice per year and given a de-worming agent, vaccines, hoof care and a complete medical evaluation. Any donkey whose health may require additional care is returned to California and our medical facilities.

Each Sanctuary has secure perimeter fencing to keep the burros contained on the property and to provide security from outside forces. It also has proper management facilities that include a collection area, sheeted alleyways and chutes for treatment.

The Plight

After many years of experience, I've learned to read a donkey's eyes. A donkey can't read, can't use a computer and can't tell you what is on television. She can, however, tell you her entire life story with just one glance. Aggression, fear, love and hate are all reflected in those large brown orbs. But she has time. With a lifespan of 40+ years, she is in no hurry to give up her secrets. She wants to tell you, but only if you have the patience to listen.

I have learned to step off the world when I am with them. It will keep spinning without me and my donkeys need someone who can give them undivided attention. Like any sensitive creature, a donkey wants you to know what she has been through. She needs to tell you that she was never given a kind word or touch and that she was left all alone with no one to talk to. But she will only tell you on her terms, in her way and only if you are willing to listen.

I have spent weeks sitting in the corner of a pen waiting for the story to unravel. One donkey had so much fear that if I approached, he would shake so violently that he would fall over. There I'd sit, paying for the sins of others, waiting for the donkey to become comfortable with me in his pen. Slowly, after several days, advancing to a hand fed carrot, "they used to beat me." A few weeks later a soft touch on the forehead, "every time someone came near me it hurt." Much later a brush stroke on the back, "they threw rocks at me when I brayed." These are just a few of the stories I've heard from the donkeys in my care.

Donkeys are by far the most mistreated domestic farm animals in America. The abuse and neglect inflicted on these animals ranges from overgrown hooves to savage beatings. Because of their limited numbers, the abuse is less noticeable than if it was inflicted on horses. Donkeys require vaccinations, hoof care, worming and a select diet, yet most receive none of these things. Many are left to fend for themselves in fields or in cramped pens. When the owner can no longer tolerate the beast he has created, it is shipped off to auction or an even worse fate.

As I ponder my purpose for writing this book, the many donkeys that I have rescued parade through my mind. They have all shared their stories with me, each one a unique tale of hardship and endurance. I have spent countless hours talking to them, listening to them and just looking into their eyes. We have saved the lives of so many animals, but there is no shortage of animals in need. So, the purpose of this book is to extend a hand to you. Talking With Donkeys is a very personal journey through the ups and downs of rescuing donkeys. These intelligent and affectionate animals forced me to rethink myself and I am a much better person for it. I sincerely hope their lessons have done the same for you.

Rescuing The Rescuers

I get so many requests for information on how to start an animal rescue that I have considered writing a book. The necessary business and legal knowledge alone could fill volumes, but that isn't what people need to know. Before doing anything else, they need to look at themselves and see if they are really suited to rescue anything.

I think that many people want to rescue animals to fill a void in their life. People, especially in the United States, have the fast food mentality of, "I want it and I get it. If it doesn't work, then I throw it away and get another one." This is one of the main reasons why animals need to be rescued in the first place. Approaching animal rescue with this attitude is not going to help anyone.

People can rescue animals without starting their own animal rescue. Local animal shelters have countless animals in desperate need of good homes and they can always use volunteers. By helping at existing rescues, you can see firsthand the heartbreak, the long hours and the sac-

rifices required when working with needy animals.

Usually this advice falls on deaf ears. They are in love with the 'idea' of running a rescue and believe that love alone will get them through. So, just to get them thinking, I like to ask the following questions:

- What do you want to rescue?
- Why do these animals need to be rescued?
- How many animals will you take care of at one time?
- Will you sell, adopt or keep all of the rescued animals? Why?
- Who are the people abusing or neglecting these animals?
- How will you prevent this abuse or neglect in the future?
- How will you ensure that you have the time and money to properly care for your animals?
- Who can you depend on to help you no matter how tough things get?
- What will happen to the animals if you die suddenly?

The idea of animal rescue is far more romantic than the actual work. Shoveling crap, treating infected wounds, picking vomit out of your hair and crying while you comfort an abused animal in the last moments of its life, are what you spend most of your time doing. It is physically demanding. Try holding 650-pound donkeys still while Doc sedates them. It is mentally demanding to stay on top of accounting, promotions, and planning. And it is emotionally draining with the constant barrage of sickness, disease, neglect and other atrocities heaped on these poor animals by a society that does not care.

All too often, people with really big hearts will start a rescue and fail miserably. They take on too much with too little knowledge and resources and the animals are the ones who suffer the most. PVDR has rescued many donkeys from other 'rescues' that were guilty of neglect because they were unable to provide even basic care. It costs PVDR more than $20,000 a month for hay and medical treatments alone. While my love for our animals is endless, love alone does not fill a hungry donkey's belly. Knowing your limitations is the key to not getting in over your head.

I was once quoted in a newspaper as saying, "Rescue without education is a complete waste of time." I got a lot of angry letters over that one, I assure you. But I stand by my statement. Abused animals exist because people abuse them. If all we do is clean up the mess, we are just enabling more abuse to take place. I have eased the suffering of thousands of animals but there are still millions out there in desperate need of help. We have to stop the abuse and to do this we must make the problem known and offer genuine solutions.

And what about plan 'B'?.Retirement, divorce, death. No one, especially in our society, wants to think about dying, but all of us will. Who will step in and keep your rescue going? Who will dedicate as much time and effort as you? These are things that most people never consider.

I often remind myself and those that work with me of my impending death. It may be tomorrow, next week or in fifty years, but I will not always be here to speak up, motivate and raise hell. My greatest fear is not my own death, but that my cause—my beloved Rescue—will die with me. So, Amy and I have taken many steps to ensure that the rescue will outlive us. We both carry 'Key Man' life insurance with the Rescue named as the beneficiary. This will provide money to hire replacements, stabilize the finances and maintain a sense of security during difficult times. We have written policies to govern every aspect of the Rescue's operations. Finally, I have instilled in my sons the desire to carry on the mission. Even at a young age, they truly understand why we exist. It is my dream that this will ensure the Peaceful Valley Donkey Rescue's continuation for generations to come.

So please, rescue to your hearts content, but do it responsibly and within your means.

What are You Willing To Sacrifice?

Another question that I get asked often is: How did you do it? How did you build a Rescue so big and so unlike anything that has ever been done before?

The only real answer is: Sacrifice.

I have put, for better or for worse, this Rescue above everything else in my life. Ahead of myself, ahead of my health, ahead of my marriage, ahead of my wife, ahead of my children and ahead of everything else. That gasp you just heard was my Mother's reaction to this statement. Unfortunately it is true. But just as unfortunate, it was necessary.

You can't make an omelet without breaking a few eggs. Well, that one is all too true. Our National Expansion is a perfect example of the sacrifice we have had to make. I am a full time resident of the state of Texas, while my wife and kids are living in California. I live alone with my two dogs. Many of the people of the small town of Miles, where I live, think that I am gay. I moved here from California, am over forty, live alone and my home is extremely neat. While I am here, I have missed Josh's basketball games, Jake's music performances and I almost missed our 16th wedding anniversary. My truck broke down in Deming, New Mexico, again, and I didn't get back to California until 11:55 pm.

I have sacrificed friends at the alter of this Rescue. Close friends that I brought in to help. Friends that I thought had certain qualities and skills that would have been beneficial to the Rescue. But these same friends lacked the drive and motivation. They didn't understand sacrifice, they looked at the Rescue as just another job. I can't blame them for that, but I also can't forgive them either.

Sometimes I imagine the Rescue is a giant boulder that I am trying to roll up a hill. Sometimes it is just Amy and I pushing, sometimes other people are standing with us, some pushing harder than others. And sometimes the boulder rolls backwards a little, crushing a few as it goes along.

I am not seeking sympathy. The decisions are mine, and I stand by them as does my family. Time away from Amy makes our kisses even more passionate, conversations with my sons more in-depth, time with my granddaughter even more enjoyable. This time apart has made us closer and more in-tune to each other. The loneliness is simply the penance I have to pay to make it work and grow this Rescue. When we are done, we will have made a difference. Not only to a hand full of animals but to an entire species. Regardless of our belief in an afterlife, a rainbow bridge or sudden darkness, we can all agree that our time here is short. I intend to use mine to make a lasting difference.

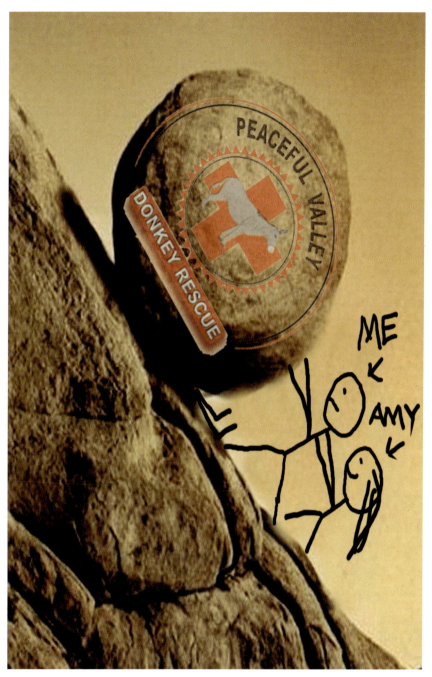

Sorry, I had a very limited special effects budget.

Why Do People Abuse Donkeys?

In a donkey rescue organization two questions pop up in every conversation: "Why do donkeys need rescuing" and "Why do people abuse donkeys"? The first question is usually answered by an introduction to the hundreds of donkeys at our rescue. The second question however, has always been a tough one to answer. Who can truly understand the human mind? How can we broad brush everyone? What separates those who handle animals roughly from those who inflict abuse? How can one truly explain the motivation behind abuse?

The answer came one Saturday afternoon while giving a tour of the rescue to a church group. The kids and parents alike genuinely enjoyed the donkeys. They saw how lovable and sweet these animals were. They remarked on how gentle and quiet they were with even the smallest of the children. They saw first hand the fear and aggression in the abused donkeys. They saw the scars, the split ears, the lumps, the bruises and the cut noses. They were able, for the first time in many of their lives, to see firsthand the result of cruelty that no animal should ever have to face.

After the tour, the Pastor made the remark that the donkey was the only mammal in the bible to be given the power of human speech. I was amazed! I had heard the stories in Sunday School, even read the bible a time or two, but how could I have forgotten this? Embarrassed, I asked to know more. I thought that this might make an interesting addition to my tours, lectures and arguments. What I heard went much deeper than an amusing anecdote, what I heard answered the age old question, "Why do people abuse donkeys?"

Numbers 22:21

Balaam, a prophet of God, was employed by some local rich folks to speak out against Israel. He saddled up his donkey and began a trip to Kirjathhuzoth. God was really upset that Balaam was going against his wishes and sent an angel to stop him. As the man and donkey traveled down a road the donkey saw the angel in front of her and turned away.

Angry at her apparent misbehavior, Balaam whipped the donkey. Again the pair traveled on until the donkey once again saw the angel blocking the road. Again she turned away and again she was whipped.

Once their journey resumed, the angel blocked a narrow passage between two walls and as the donkey turned away, she crushed Balaam's foot against the wall. As the donkey could not get away from the angel, she simply laid down. Balaam was outraged by this transgression and whipped the donkey without mercy.

As God saw this taking place, He gave the donkey the gift of speech. The donkey said, in only the way a donkey could, "Why are you beating me? Am I not the same donkey that has been faithful to you all of these years? Am I not the same donkey who has always taken you wherever you wanted to go? Why are you beating me?"

And Balaam replied, "Because you made me look stupid".

The story goes on the say that the angel appeared to Balaam and explained to him that if the donkey had not turned away he would have killed him. And Balaam saw the error of his ways and they all lived happily ever after.

But...........I had the answer! I was amazed at its simplicity and honesty. I had always searched for a deeper meaning; perhaps a genetic deficiency, or eating paint chips as children, or too much fast food and television. But it was none of these things. It was something simpler, something that weak people have no tolerance for and ignorant people lash out at. The one thing that attacks us as the "superior" being.

Question: Why do people abuse donkey?
Answer: Because they make us look stupid.

No other animal that I have ever come across has the ability to take all of your power away like a donkey. In a parade one of my donkeys stopped and would not move. On a pack trip 2 of my donkeys decided that it was time to stop after just 2 hours of hiking. In both cases I was powerless. They had all of the control over the situation. If a donkey makes a decision, he will stand by it until the end. The only way to get him to change his decision is to make him think that he has had a better idea.

You cannot force a donkey to do anything. Beating him will only make him more persistent. More persistent leads to more frustration on the part of the abuser. More frustration leads to more beating. You can beat most animals into doing anything including killing themselves. You cannot do this to a donkey. Simply stated, they make us look stupid.

Eventually, we resumed the parade route as well as the pack trip. In both cases, the donkeys simply had made a new decision and all was well in their world once again. As I enjoy these particular traits of my donkeys, I never get frustrated with it. Many times I take the opportunity to sit back and reflect on what may lie in my path (life) that may be blocking my way.

Eating Burros

"Don't let your Bulldog mouth out talk your Pekinese ass," was one of my father's favorite lines. Simply put: Don't say something unless you can back it up!

In 1971, Congress passed the Free Roaming Wild Horse and Burro Act that protected wild horses and burros on federal land regulated by the Bureau of Land Management (BLM). This protection did not extend to lands administrated by the National Park Service or the US Fish and Wildlife Service. This Act forced the BLM to conduct roundups in order to control population levels of the various herds within their jurisdiction. These animals, once caught, were then made available to the public for adoption.

In 2004, President George W. Bush, signed a revision to this Act that removed protection from many of the wild horses and burros. This new 'sale' legislation forces the BLM to sell any wild horse or burro that is ten or more years old or any animal that has been offered for adoption three times unsuccessfully. This new legislation is a death sentence for many unfortunate horses and burros. Many of the animals affected by this bill end up as food for countries in Europe and Asia.

These animals, the direct descendants of the horses and donkeys that made our great westward expansion possible, are the property of the citizens of the United States. The government's role is to protect our assets and history, not to exploit them. The thought of our noble wild horse and burro herds being eaten is unacceptable.

As the 'dominant' species, we should be ashamed of ourselves. These magnificent creatures have carved out an existence in the harshest of environments. They have kept their bloodlines strong and have adapted to a place where few others can live. Then humans enter the picture and chase, rope and trap them so they can end up in cages, awaiting their turn to be slaughtered.

When President Bush signed legislation that removed federal protection for older burros, I was infuriated. These old burros, 10+ years old, were the epitome of American Strength. They had not only survived, but flourished in the harshest place in the world. And to what end? To become dog food by the swipe of a politicians pen. So, when I received the news that burros were on their way to slaughter, I called all of my government contacts and put it on the table. The Peaceful Valley Donkey Rescue would take all of the burros that would otherwise go to the slaughterhouse.

At first, they came a few at a time. Seven in Ridgecrest. Thirteen in Kingman. No big deal. Then a call came from a holding facility in Nevada. One hundred wild burros had to go, that was the law. If we did not take them, their wretched fate was assured. So, once again, my bulldog mouth said, "YES." We called in everyone with a pair of hands to help prepare the ranch for their arrival. In addition to the 100 adults, there we going to be eight babies. While these newborns would not have gone to slaughter, they would have been separated from their mothers. That was unacceptable, so we welcomed them too.

This arrival could not have come at a worse time for the Rescue. We were spread thin from the care and management of the hundreds of donkeys already here at the time, as well as the ongoing construction of the new ranches. The burden of fundraising, taxes, employees, feed and everything else was already overwhelming. The easy answer would definitely have been "NO!" But, like I always tell my staff, "If we don't do it, who will?" Being the largest rescue in the country comes with a certain amount of responsibility in these matters. We are the only rescue in the country that can accommodate this size herd. We have the space, the staff and the expertise. All we needed were the funds.

Once all of the new burros were unloaded into their holding facilities, we began the process of castration. Typically, we can geld 13-16 whole jacks in a day. This proved to be an impossible task with this group. These burros, unlike the ones we capture, had been chased, roped, dragged and shocked. When we put them in our old alleyway, they would jump, kick and bite! As it is my job to restrain the donkeys while Dr. John sedates them, I was getting beat up. They proved to be so difficult to handle that we were only able to castrate six. A new all time low!

I made the decision that we were going to put the castrations on hold until we were better equipped to handle these rowdy boys. We designed and built a new section of secure holding pens, alleyways, crowding tubs and squeeze chutes. The cost was extremely high, but we felt that it was the only way to safely handle donkeys that had been soured on people. I also have a fear that one day I will not be able to rebound from the injuries that come with my profession. If I am unable to continue, who will step up to replace me? Our new system has simplified our work and enabled more people to safely assist.

We also received many pregnant jennets in that group. With the arrival of spring, babies were being born right on nature's schedule. We probably ended up with at least 18 newborns. An added difficulty with this group, however, is that the moms are so untrusting of humans that they instill this mistrust in their offspring. The staff and I really have our work cut out for us in gentling both moms and babies.

As the jacks settle down and the babies get older, they will all be introduced into one of the herd groups on the ranch. In a few years, even the meanest of the bunch will learn to trust me. I sometimes wonder what would have happened if we just let them all go to slaughter. Would that have stirred interest in the Plight of the American Donkey? By accepting this burden, have we allowed sleazy politicians to slink past yet another scandal? Perhaps. But we now have another 100+ wonderful animals at the Rescue that matter a lot more to me than politics.

Texas Burro Project

A while back, I was getting into the shower, there was a knock at the bathroom door. Larry had made a mad dash into the house and was desperately searching for me. As I opened the door I saw Josh, my son, holding an excited Larry. For those who do not know Larry, he is a Jack Russell Terrier and he has been on more adventures in his five years than most people have in their entire lifetime. As I looked him over I decided that he could use a shower as well. So as we have done hundreds of times in showers, lakes, streams and with heated water from a pot in the middle of some remote desert, Larry and I cleaned up. Later, as he and I sat in my armchair with him wrapped in a warm blanket, I looked at Amy and said "A clean Larry can only mean one thing…I must have a road trip coming."

As fate would have it, the next day I received a call from the Texas Parks and Wildlife Department. They wanted us to get involved with their burro herd on the Big Bend Ranch State Park. They have been trying to reduce the numbers of wild burros on the park by shooting them, close to 100 have already been killed. This method of reduction was not working and they had started to get bad press from the shootings. They had tried capture programs but they proved costly and ineffectual as well. I knew about the Big Bend Ranch burros long before the call ever came through. You see, as stories circulate around the Internet most people forward them to me, so that I can fix the problem. Unfortunately for me, I have no one else to forward them to. "The buck stops here", "If not us than who?" It seems redundant, but as always it all comes down to Peaceful Valley.

Most people's reaction to hearing that a hundred burros have been shot is outrage and disgust. My reaction however is a little different. When I hear of the destruction of wild burros, I feel lonely, tired, and broken. You see, I know that the government shoots burros as part of the solution to a problem. Animal activists attack the solution without replacing it with another. As an animal rescuer I have to be a little more reasonable than that. If we are going to stop the shootings, we have to replace it with a solution the includes capturing them. I know all too well that this means months away from my family. Cold nights sleeping under bushes. Granola bars and dirty water. Not getting to see Josh play basketball or Jake play drums in a concert. I don't have the luxury of feeling outrage or disgust, I am too busy trying to solve the problem.

As I hung up the phone with the Texas Park's Regional Director, I told Amy what we were up against. Like me, Amy knew in an instant what this would mean in financial costs, hardship and time apart. One benefit of being married for a long time is that you can have an entire conversation without ever uttering a word. A slight smile, watery eyes and a nod was all the confirmation I needed to know that she would do her

My ancestors have been here
for over 400 years.

We have made our home in
the harshest parts of this
country, trying to avoid
you.

Over time, your
people have
polluted the
waters, air
and soil.

You have taken
what was beauti-
ful and allowed
your greed to
make it ugly.

You have destroyed every
thing that has been in
your way...
now you say it is our turn.

Peaceful Valley Donkey Rescue
The voice for those who cannot speak
for themselves.

www.donkeyrescue.org

The Crazy VooDoo Lady

On my first visit to Big Bend Ranch, I was taken on a tour of the burro areas by Texas Parks and Wildlife Regional Director Mike Hill. We spent a few days traveling the park and getting to know one another.

While I was on this trip I was updating the blog on our website and made mention that I liked Mike. Mike is a Viet Nam Veteran that still carries the wound that he received in battle. He is originally from California and he and I were familiar with many of the same places. Mike is a real person, the kind that are few and far between.

After posting my message on the blog, I received one of the most hate filled e-mails imaginable. Now I am a pretty good judge of hate filled emails because I get so many. It seems I can't go a day without upsetting someone. She was upset that I liked Mike, because Mike was one of the shooters that had killed the burros in the park. And because I liked him, I was no better than he was. She went on to say that she sincerely hoped that the remainder of my days would be filled with misery and I would suffer more than the burros who were killed.

Wow! Now the thing that made me the maddest was the threat. I don't expect people to agree with me, everyone has the right to be wrong and people who disagree with me usually are. But the two things I do not take are advice and threats, especially when they are given over the e-mail. People get a lot braver on a keyboard than they ever would in my face.

I like Mike Hill, but I do not like his job. I do not like or agree with the TPWD's plan for the Big Bend Ranch. I would much rather see the entire 300,000 acres turned into the world's largest Burro Reserve. I would be king and I would rule with a gentle and fatherly hand. We would have an open borders policy so that any Mexican Burro could come and visit their Northern Cousins. These Mexican burros would not become citizens of my Burro Utopia but would be allowed to legally stay as long as they stayed out of trouble and contributed to the common good. We would have a reasonable priced health-care system provided by non-profits, not a greed based or government controlled one. We would have an election system that didn't require huge contributions from special interest groups and therefore the burro politicians would truly represent their constituents and not the people who bought them off. But no one asked for my opinion.

My job is not to fight with the government. My job is to save burros. I have studied far too much history to want to fight the United States government on any issue. Peaceful Valley is welcomed into these types of programs because we are professional. Professionals that catch, treat, gentle and adopt out domestic donkeys and wild burros. We have done it more than anyone else.

Things That Go Bump In The Night

When I am home in my comfortable chair sipping a glass of red wine and reading a good book, I long for the chance to get back to the desert, back to catching wild burros. It is funny how romantic things seem when you are away from them. I talk to people so often about my burro catching adventures that I can't wait to get back out there. But once I get there, I remember the other side to burro capture. The side that is not very romantic. The side where it is lonely, boring, hot, dusty and you don't get much sleep.

Many of our capture programs begin with me hiking around an area, often times never actually seeing a burro. I am looking for trails, droppings and places where they congregate and roll in the dust. I make notes, jot down GPS coordinates and plan trap locations. If I find an exceptional area, I might leave some hay to keep the burros close. These days are long and hard, a lot of hiking and a lot of climbing.

Once I have a pretty good feel for how many burros are in the area and at what intervals they come through there, I will set my trap. The trap is nothing fancy, corral panels and a self closing gate. The trick is to get the burros to enter and stay in until I come back to pick them up. In other places, I close the trap myself. I will place one of my donkeys in the trap to lure the wild burros in. Once inside I pull the rope from my place of concealment and the spring loaded gate is released.

In Texas, where our current program is in full swing, I spend a lot of time working alone. Hiding under bushes, lurking around trees and crouching behind boulders with my cowboy hat on my head and my .357 revolver on my hip, I must look like a bald headed Walker Texas Ranger. Often times I don't catch anything, other times I catch too many. It is kind of like fishing above the water. There are so many factors to consider, sometimes you forget one and the burros slip away.

This particular area along the Mexican Border has obvious signs of drug trafficking. Tire tracks crossing the shallow Rio Grande over to the US side, the tire tracks ending up a sandy canyon and the footprints of a teenage boy continuing on. The boys carry the drugs in backpacks for many miles in order to get past the border checkpoints and avoid detection. This kind of smuggling has been going on for hundreds of years, it is a way of life and one of the few jobs available.

On one particularly dark moonless night, I was in my hiding place overlooking my trap. The burros had been seen in this area very near the road that parallels the Rio Grande. Around 1:00 am a pickup truck drove slowly by, obviously looking over my trap, and then drove on out of sight. A few minutes later, the same truck came by, this time even slower. Now the thing to remember is that this area of Texas is empty and without law enforcement. There is no cell service and even if there was, there wouldn't be any one to call. It is just me, Larry, the burros and sometimes the bad guys.

On the pickup's third pass by the trap, I emerged from my place of concealment with my revolver in my hand. I walked steadily towards the truck. When the two men inside saw what I was carrying, they quickly accelerated the truck and disappeared from sight. I never saw them again that evening.

Around 3:00 am, I heard the patter of little feet on the highway heading towards me. I immediately knew the sound, it was Larry. He had been sleeping in my truck that was parked half of a mile away so that it wouldn't scare the burros. Distant thunder was enough to dislodge Larry from the truck, he always has hated storms. Fortunately for Larry, I keep the back window open a little and the truck does not have a tailgate so he can get in and out of the truck on his own. (There is a funny story as to why most of my trucks do not have tailgates, but I will save that for another edition).

So Larry and I settled into my folding chair. I didn't have much hope for catching burros that night so I let myself drop off into sleep, Larry snoozing on my chest. At some point, I heard Izzy let out a very aggressive snort from the trap. Izzy is the perfect trap donkey because she loves company and will bray all night to attract burros. This snort however, was very out of character. I stayed reclined in my chair, but I listened intently to try and determine what she was upset about.

Then I heard it, a low 'hungh', again a little louder 'hungh', still louder 'hungh'. With a sudden snap of realization I leapt from my chair and grabbed the flashlight that was on my right side. As the beam of light swept upward, it caught the gleam of two, tiny black eyes and a snout with razor sharp tusks. A javelina was standing not three feet away from me. Fortunately no one was around to hear because a shrill scream came out of me, like nothing that I have uttered in my life. The javelina, apparently just as surprised as I was, let out a scream of his own, I ran up the hill and he ran down. By the time I stopped running and turned back, the javelina was no where in sight. After I caught my breath and regained my senses, I realized that the javelina was probably tracking Larry. Javelina have no love for dogs and will kill them if they get the opportunity. The javelina had picked up Larry's scent on the highway and it led him directly to me.

Where was Larry during this whole javelina episode you may ask? At some point between me screaming like a little girl and then running up the hill, Larry had bolted back to the safety of the truck. He jumped into the bed, crawled through the open window and hid on the floorboards of the front seat. Larry might be a great conversationalist and even tell a decent joke once in awhile, but he ain't much for protection.

Javelina — Texas Parks and Wildlife Division Photo

Larry

Hell No, Those Are Amy's Pigs!

Even though the sign on the door says Donkey Rescue, from time to time we have taken in other species as well. Many of these came as part of a donkey rescue. How can we take donkeys out of these terrible situation and leave other animals behind to suffer? That is how our Forgotten Animal Sanctuary was born. As it has grown, many other things have found their way into the protection of our sanctuary.

At the Forgotten Animal Sanctuary, we get all types of animals. Most represent society's endless demand for new and exciting pets. These animals are nothing more than a fad, and like all fads, they fade into obscurity as quickly as they arrived. When was the last time you consulted your Mood Ring or held your Cabbage Patch Kid? Here today, gone tomorrow. As many people discover, however, you cannot hide unwanted animals in the attic with your pet rock and parachute pants.

Pot Bellied Pigs were a huge item in the 1990s. Everyone wanted one and this created a huge market. Breeders sprang up everywhere and with no consideration for conformation, the pig population exploded. A typical sow can have 10 piglets and can do this several times in a year. This resulted in a problem of "epig" proportions.

What most people did not realize in their zeal to be the first on the block to get a pig, was the fact that pigs are very intelligent and easily become bored. A pig can learn to use a litter box, so owners assumed it was alright to leave them at home while they were away. But the pig, once it was tired of napping, would take a stroll around the house opening cabinets and refrigerator doors. Ransacking the kitchen is fun but their real enjoyment came from rooting underneath the linoleum. Many a pig owner would come home to a fat pig and a destroyed house.

It's no surprise that many pet pigs were relocated to the back yard, but that wasn't a safe move either. Rooting, scratching and leaning on fences, the demolition was never ending. But what was a frustrated pig owner to do? Usually a pig yard with doghouse was constructed and the pig was forgotten about, or worse, it was dropped off at the County Shelter.

I have often said, "Show me a fad concerning animals and I will show you the need for a rescue!" As a result of the pig fad, several Pot Bellied Pig rescues popped up around the country. Some faired better than others, but there always seemed to be more pigs than places to put them. Some of the former pets were just set free to fend for themselves.

We at PVDR receive several calls each year regarding pig rescue. Unless the situation is dire, we try to route the call to someone else who might be interested in helping. But there are some situations, usually concerning older or aggressive pigs, in which Amy and I will perform the rescue ourselves. We have taken pigs from junkyards, backyards, breed-

Keswick, the ugliest pig in the world

ing mills and shelters. Most of the pigs in our care are mean, nasty and a far cry from the sweet pets that won a temporary place in the hearts of Americans.

    I have the unfortunate duty of being the "bad guy" when it comes to the pigs. I have to worm them, vaccinate them and trim their hooves. The pigs are smart enough to recognize me and go to great lengths to avoid me. And while Amy gets endless pleasure from watching me get knocked down by her pigs, I can assure you that I will never be called the Pig Man. And when you come to visit our Forgotten Animal Sanctuary and remark, "Oh look, you have pigs," my response will remain, "Hell No! Those are Amy's pigs."

Winston, caught in a junkyard

Let us use our intelligence wisely.
Otherwise, how are we superior to animals?
His Holiness the 14th Dalai Lama

Who Are You Calling Stubborn?

Amy and I were loading Rico into the trailer after an Easter performance. Rico is our go-to-guy for most church functions. I take him through his part a few times and then he is ready. He has never missed a cue and more importantly, has never tossed Jesus to the floor. Of course they made me dress up like one of the bald headed, goatee wearing wisemen. As we were loading Rico, he stood defiantly at the end of his rope refusing to get into the trailer.

"They sure are stubborn, " said a man who had driven up next to us in the parking lot.

"What would you do if I grabbed you and tried to shove you in this noisy, metal box?" I asked, unable to bite back my anger.

Trailer rides are awful. I know this because I have had to ride in horse trailers several times because of various medical conditions of the donkeys we were transporting. It is noisy, you have no control over the movement and abrupt stops can be unnerving. Rico has been in a trailer many times, enough times that he knows that he does not like it. Is Rico stubborn or is he just intelligent?

Donkeys have an over developed sense of self preservation. If they do not like something or do not feel safe doing something, then they won't. This is where they get their reputation for stubbornness. A horse, an amazingly stupid animal, can be made to do anything, including killing itself. Horses are considered noble and magnificent, donkeys are considered obstinate. If these same characteristics were addressed in people, would we hold the same opinions?

Judge Not

We give many tours at our Rescue. Some tours are for people who are interested in learning about donkeys and others are for potential adopters that are looking over the herd for a possible addition to their family. I always encourage people to come out several times to get to know the donkeys. Each donkey is unique and all of his or her individual traits should be recognized before making a choice.

I remember one woman in particular who was interested in adopting. I walked her through the ranch explaining donkey nature and pointing out different donkeys that might make suitable candidates. At each recommendation, she would point out a physical flaw. That one is too fat. That one is too skinny. That one has too many scars. That one has a chunk missing from its ear. That one has crooked legs. That one walks funny.

And so it went, donkey after donkey, critique after critique. I don't consider myself a good judge of character and I usually give everyone the benefit of the doubt, but this women had clearly shown me that she was too judgmental and did not deserve to have one of our donkeys. My agitation finally erupted when I almost shouted, "Of course they are not perfect, but look at you!"

In my anger at her harsh judgment of my donkeys, I desperately wanted to point to her own flaws so that she could see the hypocrisy that she was living. I wanted her to feel the pain of being unwanted because of the way she looked. I wanted her to know just how far from perfect she was so that I and my donkeys could feel vindicated. But, of course, I didn't. Trading pain for pain is never a solution. She knew how she looked. She knew how others perceived her. She knew what it meant to be judged. Maybe her being judgmental was simply a defense mechanism that she had developed over many sad years.

There is no happy conclusion to this story. She did not adopt a donkey from the Rescue and I can only hope that she found peace within herself. Always look at the heart and never the appearance. It is a sad affair that our society has created such a thin model of beauty while growing fat consuming our own hypocritical judgment of others.

The P Word

Living in Texas these past few months has cleared some of the California Cobwebs from my brain. Hardly a day goes by where I do not overhear a Texan say something that is totally politically incorrect. But over time, I have realized that its not them being Politically Incorrect, it's the California brainwashing that has made me hyper sensitive to everyone's "feelings". Texas has reminded me what America used to be like.

I received an email the other day that asked that we, meaning everyone at Peaceful Valley, stop using the P-word. It seems that the P-word is sprinkled throughout our websites and printed literature. And much to this person's disgust, I have even said it on television. As long as we use the P-word, there will never be a chance at true equality and our "companion animals" will continue to live as property in a total pit of despair.

I emailed this person back and asked if she was serious. I admit that we use the P-word but never in a derogatory manner. Our field trips revolve around a central theme of Responsible P-word Ownership, we have a Educational P-word Shop where kids learn that animals are not impulse buys and are not disposable. We also teach children that animals in the Exotic P-word Trade do not make good P-words and usually end up neglected or euthanized.

Well, she did not see the humor in my response. She went on to say that using the P-word to describe companion animals was just as bad as using the N-word to describe blacks. Now upon receiving this comparison, I quickly ended our online email debate because I was going to have to use the F-word. Comparing the word Pet, (oops I said it) to racial slurs is just stupid. Try focusing your attention on pet overpopulation or dog fighting or animal cruelty. Wasting your efforts on trying to get people who actually care for animals to stop using the word pet…well that's just BS-word!

The United States was once a world leader. We set the precedence for freedom and democracy coupled with the strength to protect it. I am afraid that those days are dying. We have been made to feel guilty for everything and to be ashamed of our accomplishments as a nation.

Congress recently apologized for slavery. In all of my life, I have never met anyone who thought slavery was a good idea. I do not recall, ever once, someone saying that they were proud of our slavery past. And when you realize that no one from our slavery past is still alive, but the majority of our orange juice is picked by our slavery present, who are we apologizing to?

In the 21st Century, China and Russia will become the world powers. They are aggressive, financially stable and have their eye on the prize. We here in America are broke, our money is almost valueless, all of our good companies are owned by foreigners, we import almost a trillion dollars worth of fuel each year, and what do we do? Worry about words.

Rawhide Memorial Ranch & Sanctuary

The Tehachapi Ranch is our largest facility and is home to our Corporate Headquarters. Located in the Tehachapi Mountains, this facility can accommodate several hundred donkeys as well as other hoof stock animals. Tehachapi handles all of our Western Division and is our main medical facility.

Location:	Tehachapi, CA
Coordinates:	35D 09'40.35" N 118D 19'31.50" W Elv 4,138
Acreage:	140
Distances To:	Miles, TX 1,297 miles Mineral, VA 2,559 miles
Approximate Capacity:	600 large animals
Handicap Accessible:	yes
Features:	Gift Shop, Visitor Center, Faux Pet Shop, Self Guided Driving/Walking Tours

George Blumentritt Memorial Ranch

The Texas Burro Rescue is our operating name in the State of Texas. The ranch facility is located on a former cotton farm. This facility is designed to handle approximately 250 wild burros and domestic donkeys and can be managed by just one person. The Texas facility handles all of the Central Division and acts as a layover for our donkeys traveling across the country.

Location:	Miles, TX
Coordinates:	31D 35'40.01" N 100D 10'02.62" W Elv 1,788'
Acreage:	65
Distances To:	Tehachapi, CA 1,297 miles Mineral, VA 1,496 miles
Approximate Capacity:	250 large animals
Handicap Accessible:	yes
Features:	Guided Tours

Mineral Virginia
Olde Towne Farm

Peaceful Valley's East Coast facility is located on a former cattle ranch in Mineral, VA. This facility has several large grassy pastures, three barns and equipment sheds. Located in the middle of the eastern seaboard, this facility handles all of our Eastern Division.

Location:	Mineral, VA
Coordinates:	38D 00'57.59" N 77D 53'11.06" W Elv 416'
Acreage:	100
Distances To:	Tehachapi, CA 2,559 miles Miles, TX 1,496 miles
Approximate Capacity:	400 large animals
Handicap Accessible:	yes
Features:	Guided Tours

We see.
We hear.
We feel.
We matter.

Please join the fight to protect us.

Peaceful Valley
Donkey Rescue

www.donkeyrescue.org

Making A Real Difference

Many years ago, I was quoted in a newspaper as saying that my life-long goal was to "Improve The Plight of the American Donkey." If you have visited our websites, read our books or visited our ranch you are probably very familiar with this statement. It is my mantra, it is what I believe in, it is what I have always worked for.

A few years later I was interviewed for the LA Times and was asked if I thought I was making a difference. My response was "No, these few donkeys represent only the tip of a very large iceberg of abuse, neglect and mismanagement."

Today…well today…things are a little different!

Today, Peaceful Valley has three corporate ranches one located in Tehachapi California, one in Miles Texas, and a third in Mineral Virginia. All three are staffed by professionally trained and experienced staff. All are capable of rescuing, doctoring, training and adopting donkeys.

We have many adoption centers located across the country. These adoption centers allow for our donkeys to not only be placed in loving homes, but be watched over by our staff and volunteers in each area. These locations also act as satellite rescue facilities to bring in donkeys that need help. These donkeys are then transported to one of the Corporate Ranches for treatment and care. Our Adoption Centers are located from the Pacific North West all the way to the Florida Coast.

We have distributed 5,000 copies of our Care and Feeding Book throughout the country. These books are an invaluable resource to donkey owners and with the knowledge that we are sharing, we are preventing future abuse and neglect from ever happening. With these books we are changing the way donkeys are handled, fed and castrated.

We have hosted thousands of school age children in our Compassionate Learning Center Field Trip Program. Children of all ages learn the responsibility that goes along with animal ownership. They also learn the true meaning of compassion and how to apply it to each other, animals and the planet.

We have established working relationships with the Bureau of Land Management, the National Park Service, US Fish and Wildlife as well as many State, County and City organizations. We receive calls from all over the United States to assist in donkey related matters.

We have changed the way donkeys are viewed with our television shows, radio interviews, newspaper and magazine articles, our books and our nationwide speaking appearances.

So it is with great pride and teary eyes, that I can honestly say that we are finally Improving The Plight of the American Donkey. But our work is far from done. Simply having the 'machine' in place does not get the work done. Now, more than ever, we need your help. Many rescues are folding up and their animals are suffering as a result of our economy. And while you will never receive a desperate plea from us, please know that times are tough for us as well. Our hay cost per ton has doubled in the last few years and we all know the current fuel price. While most rescues devote their resources to saving a few animals right now, Peaceful Valley is looking towards the future.

Peaceful Valley is here for the long haul. We are a professional organization and we intend to be here for as long as there are donkeys suffering. But we are dependant on your generosity.

Please stand with us as we make a real difference, not just to "some animals" but to an entire species.

Part 3
THE BURROMAN

The success of Peaceful Valley is directly related to my vision, direction, unabashed profanity and brute force. I have built and operated my rescue with the same principles that govern my life: Honesty, Sincerity and Strength. I am deeply appreciative of the people who have helped to make Peaceful Valley what it is today, and more importantly what it will become tomorrow.

In this section I would like to share some of my personal philosophies. Take away only those things that you agree with, leave the rest on these pages.

Even with my big talk and far reaching plans, it is important to remember why we rescue. If we forget to have compassion for all of them, then we have accomplished nothing.

The starfish story is my constant reminder of why we do what we do.

As a man took an early morning walk along a beach, he saw that thousands of starfish had been stranded on shore by the thrashing waves of a violent storm the night before. He then noticed a boy tossing the starfish, one by one, back into the water.

"What are you doing?" asked the man.

"Saving these starfish. If they don't get back into the water, they will die," replied the boy.

"But there are too many. How could you ever hope to make a difference?"

The boy reached down, picked up another starfish and threw it into the water. "I just made a huge difference to that one."

The Great Sheep Story

Some people say there are two sides to every story and that truth is often just a matter of perspective. What a load of crap! There is only one truth and the truth is usually found in the best story. Fact is fact and everything else is...well, just plain wrong. I mention this only because Amy and I usually see eye to eye, but a recent event has us going head to head. You, the unbiased and intelligent reader, can settle this dispute once and for all.

Here is the story...
Every three months, we are faced with the enormous task of de-forming all of the hundreds of animals on the ranches. The donkeys receive an awful tasting oral paste. (Please don't ask me how I came by this knowledge.) Our sheep receive their de-worming by injection, which means that Amy and I have to go into the sheep pen and catch each individual animal. We have many breeds of sheep at the Rescue, everything from tiny sweet-faced sheep to huge ferocious creatures that can weigh more than one hundred pounds.

As you may know, sheep are flock animals. Which means that when they sense danger, they huddle together for safety. So, as Amy and I try to catch one animal, the flock is doing everything in their power to stay together and away from us. Needless to say, catching sheep is challenging work.

On this particular occasion, we were down to our last animal. But this was no ordinary ewe—she was gargantuan by sheep standards. We had her cornered but her stance told us she was not going to be an easy catch. Our plan was to slowly close in and when the time was right, I would yell, "Now!" and we would rush in and grab her. It is important to remember, however, that this giant ewe's goal in life was to rejoin the flock behind us.

Unexpectedly, she made the first move. With determination in her eyes, she leaped into the air like one of Santa's reindeer and hit me square in the chest. Her momentum caused me to fall backwards. We now come to the point of the story where Amy and I can't seem to agree. Amy's fairy tale account, as the intelligent reader will plainly observe, does not agree with the known facts. But, again, you be the judge.

Amy's version goes something like, "This cute little sheep knocked big, macho Mark flat on his butt and it was dumb luck that his hand got tangled in her wool and slowed her down long enough for me to catch her. I had already administered the injection by the time he came to his senses and blah, blah, blah."

This is how it really happened: As I stood in my best sheep catching stance, my keen senses warned me that my opponent was about to launch a counter attack. I made the split-second decision to use my opponent's energy against her. As she rammed her massive frame into my chest, I expertly flipped myself backwards using my cat-like reflexes and everything I ever learned from watching Andre the Giant. As our airborne bodies neared the ground, I carefully wrapped my fingers tightly around her wool. To the uneducated, it may have looked like I hit the ground with a thud, but it was actually a highly specialized maneuver to flip the gigantic creature over my head and safely to the ground. Once there, I held her immobile until my meek assistant could stop laughing in obvious fear and muster enough courage to join in.

I think the truth is obvious.

Jasper

Jasper was an owner-surrender from the San Diego area of Southern California. Along with two jennets, he had been rescued from a horrible situation by the person that was giving them to us. All three donkeys wore their abuse in different ways. Honey Buns was withdrawn and timid around people. She would frantically run from anything walking on two legs and showed little interest in ever becoming people-friendly. Julie was simple minded. She had scars and abnormalities on her head that were more than likely the result of many severe beatings. Jasper was different.

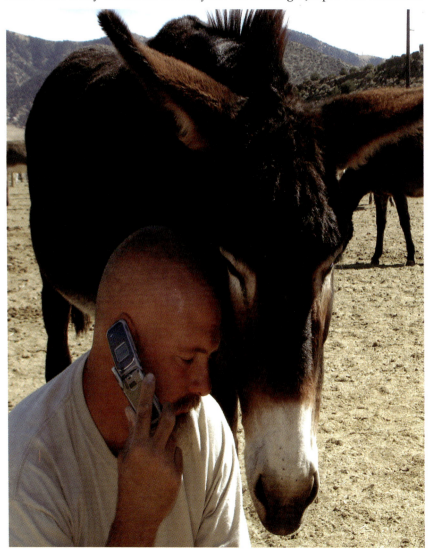

He was not shy, timid, or scared. He was mad.

Jasper had been subjected to numerous savage beatings at the hands of his previous owner. Because he knew that human approach meant pain, he reacted by trying to inflict a little of his own. When I would walk up to his pen, he would charge to within a few feet of the bars, snort and paw at the ground. Like a boxer in a prizefight, he would do everything in his power to intimidate his opponent. If I entered his pen, Jasper would circle around me in a frenzy throwing kicks at my head. This would continue until I had enough sense to leave. When I would exit his pen, Jasper would stop kicking, but he would continue his intimidation tactics until I left the area.

This was the routine, day after day, week after week. 'I' ran through all of 'my' experiences with other aggressive donkeys. 'I' tried to think of new methods. 'I' even consoled myself, telling myself that it wasn't 'my' fault that I was failing. But then I remembered that 'I' does not belong in the equation. This is Jasper's time. His life, experiences, likes, hates and feelings are all that matter.

Jasper reacted to people as he did because he felt threatened. He knew that people were bad and blind fury was his best defense. The only way for me to appear non-threatening was to become smaller, to act timid, to not be me. Knowing what needed to be done and mustering the courage to do it were two very different things. My wonderful wife would never have allowed me to do what had to be done, so I waited one afternoon until she left to get the kids from school.

I walked up to Jasper's pen, opened the gate, walked to the center and sat down. Because of the quickness of my movements, Jasper was unable to snort or paw at the ground. He instantly went into his kicking craze, but as soon as I sat down, he stopped. I, the human, was no longer a threat. In fact, the human was now an easy target, just as he had been as a defenseless donkey locked in a pen.

Jasper's aggression and violence arose from his indescribable abuse. His nature was not to be cruel or violent. Once the enemy was no longer a threat, he could relax and even let his guard down. He could approach the human on his own terms. He could explore and investigate at his own pace. He could begin to let go of the pain from countless savage beatings.

After many sessions, Jasper learned to forgive us for his past experiences. He became a donkey again and eventually became a friend. He is usually one of the first donkeys to greet visitors at the gate and is particularly fond of children.

Jasper had fixed himself. 'I' just had to get out of the way so that he could.

Removing The I

When I first started working with animals many years ago, I felt the need to convince. The animals in my care had been mistreated by humans and had no reason to trust anyone ever again. Years of systematic abuse and misery cannot easily be forgotten or forgiven. My job, to begin with, was to find a way to convince these poor creatures that I was different. They needed to know that I would never hurt them. The problem with my theory was that these animals did not care about me. "I" was unimportant to them. "I" was simply another human. "I" was no different than the ones who cause pain.

Many times when we work with others, we unintentionally put the focus on ourselves. As I would sit in the donkey pen, I would try my best to convince the donkeys of my pure intentions. Unfortunately, the "I" would creep forward and cloud the issues.

'I' am a donkey expert.
'I' have studied donkey nature for many years.
'I' have saved the lives of hundreds of donkeys.
'I' have been on several TV shows.

'I' needed to fall on my face a few times before I was really ready to make a difference.

When working with anyone or anything, you must remove the 'I' and focus only on the 'you'. Why are you here? What have you experienced? What do you fear? What do you like? What do you hold sacred? What do you resent? Careful and non-obtrusive observation over a long period of time has always worked best for me. Noticing reactions to different objects and scenarios makes the recovery period easier as it keeps mistakes and subsequent setbacks to a minimum.

Because many donkey abusers wear cowboy hats, some of my donkeys associated hats with pain. I could therefore save myself a lot of problems by simply not wearing a hat. Manure rakes have been used to strike donkeys, so it is best to carefully watch a donkey's reaction to the rakes before cleaning their stall.

To truly become a selfless caregiver, you must set aside all of your own wants, needs and desires. If I insisted on always wearing my hat, going about my chores a certain way, or approaching each animal in my own predictable fashion, then most of my time and energy would be wasted rescuing my own ego.

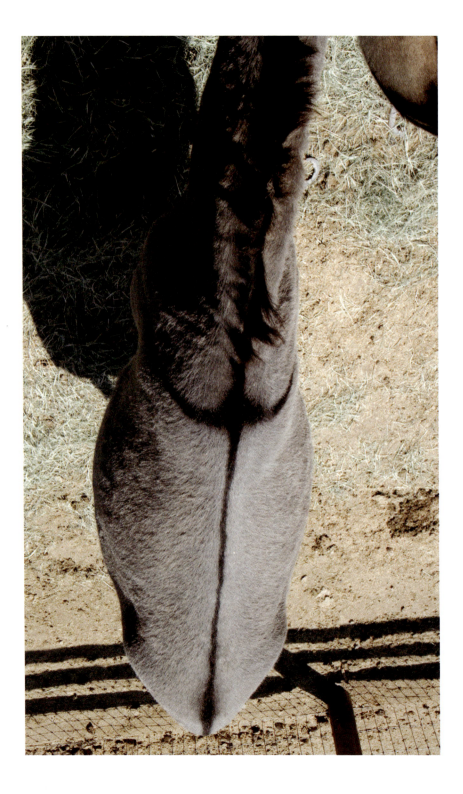

Jesus Was A Burroman

When we began the second edition project with 'Burroman' in the title, I was surprised to find that many people were unfamiliar with the stories of the burromen. As a history buff, the late 1800s and early 1900s are awash in the lore and legends of these men. They forged new trails, discovered riches and just plain survived in one of the world's harshest regions. I assumed that other people were as interested in the subject as me. Of course, I had also assumed everyone in this country had read, understood and knew the US constitution as well.

While the American burromen of the early twentieth century are the most famous burromen, it all began thousands of years ago. Egyptians first domesticated donkeys around 3000 BC, and they were used to construct the cities and wondrous monuments of that civilization. They were also used in trade, eventually being traded themselves to other cultures. As they spread throughout many regions of the world, donkeys were a key factor in the advancement of humanity and the distribution of cultural, scientific and religious ideas.

As domesticated donkeys spread, so did the spirit of the burroman. The Prophets of the Old Testament traveled on donkeys, as did the missionaries of Buddhism, Christianity and Islam. These men, atop or beside their faithful donkeys, forged new paths and beliefs wherever they traveled. In their time, they were often misunderstood, but the spirit of these brave men ensured the existence of their religions to this day.

Jesus was one of the finest members in the ranks of burromen. While the miracles attributed to him get the most attention, it was his independent spirit that truly inspired me. He was a man who stuck to his beliefs regardless of the consequences. He disregarded the established view that women were of low status and rejected dogmatic thinking. He spoke out against social injustice and shared his meals with outcasts. And, not least among his many attributes, he challenged the greatest empire on Earth with only his words and his way. And when he rode to meet his fate, it was not on the back of a horse as a fearless warrior. Instead, he rode on a humble donkey. He understood the true nature of life and death. He was a Burroman to the very end.

A Long Road To Here

I've never understood why I have to fill out so many forms when I visit the doctor's office. My insurance pays half and I pay the other half, end of story. Whether or not they know my favorite color, zodiac sign and SAT score doesn't need to enter into the transaction. Anyway, I was recently filling out the first of about twenty forms when it asked for my occupation. I answered: BURROMAN. Years earlier when asked who was my employer, I would proudly answer: ME, MYSELF & I.

I was always very proud of being self-employed and not having to rely on others to provide for my family. I knew that what we had, or didn't have, was my doing. It was this side to Amy's and my personalities that allowed us to build the Peaceful Valley Donkey Rescue. We know how to sacrifice, manage and plan. Most people would be intimidated by the risk and responsibility, but it was a natural step forward for Amy and I.

As I sat in the doctor's office with my lap full of paperwork, I thought about the path I had taken to get to this place in my life. I guess

you could say that my life flashed before my eyes.

My music career started when I was twelve years old. Playing drums at fairs, parties, BBQs and schools, I fell in love with the cheer of a crowd. I quickly learned how to work an audience to get the most laughs, the most applause and the most appreciation for my art. My teenage years had begun with great promise, but a dark cloud eventually formed around me. The music and the lifestyle of the early 80's was accompanied by bad habits and terrible choices that would haunt me for years to come.

I was only twenty years old when my first child was born and two more quickly followed. I found myself working as an electrician in a dead end job and married to a dreadful person with three kids who deserved a better life. Hardship and poverty are all we can remember of those years. But the dark clouds lifted when I finally cleaned myself up, got a long overdue divorce and custody of my children. As the kids' mother all but vanished from our lives, I vowed to never fall into that hole again.

With my new outlook on life, things improved almost overnight. I began working for a better construction company and was making decent money. We weren't rich, but the kids and I could afford to buy a pizza now and then. Despite the stress of being a single dad, I found it easier to laugh and enjoy my time with my kids. We thought life could not get any better, but we were wrong. Amy entered the picture and things got dramatically better.

Amy was a mere 18 years and 5 months old when we were married. Of course, everyone just knew that it would never work. "A marriage between a divorced twenty-seven year old with three kids and an eighteen year old babysitter will never succeed," they said. They were wrong. Amy and I found qualities in the other that we both desperately needed. Stability. Love. Honesty. We were meant for each other.

My construction career finally netted me an office job under the tutelage of one the most successful men in the construction industry. J.B. Wise was one of those bosses you hated and respected at the same time. I worked late and spent many a night in my office. I sacrificed and most importantly, I learned. I absorbed every word, every gesture and everything that I thought might make me and my family more successful. Still, no matter how hard I worked, if I fell short of my goal, J.B. would look up at me and say, "You didn't do it because you didn't care," or "There is no prize for second best." These were hard lessons, but ones that I came to understand as absolute laws. No matter what the cost, failure is not an option.

I eventually went on to own the very business that J.B. Wise had built. Through hard work and much sacrifice, Amy and I achieved what we called success. We finally had money, homes, cars and all the things we had dreamed about during the early days. But success is a double-edged sword. Business is war and no war is won without casualties. Strained family relationships, loss of friends and the endless problems of having employees all took a toll on my health. Ulcers, high blood pressure and migraines were commonplace. And for what? More money? More stuff? We decided that all the wealth in the world would never compare to the time we could be spending together. So, over a period of a few years, we closed down our businesses and committed all of our time to the Rescue.

So here I am, a full time Burroman. If any one piece of the puzzle of my life had been different, I would not be where I am today. After traveling so many roads, I often wonder what's around the corner. Whatever it is, I've never been happier than I am right now. I know that I am doing exactly what I was meant to be doing with the person I was born to love.

You Can Keep Sorry

Regardless of what we 'think' and 'feel', our lives are the sum of what we 'say' and 'do'. Our words and actions determine how others view us throughout our lifetime and, at some point, we will all say or do something that we know is wrong. Whether it is being rude to a waitress or robbing a bank, once it is done, there is no taking it back. How we respond to these mistakes is a clear mark of our character.

In our society, and probably many others, no one wants to take the blame for their own actions. If a mistake is made, the first thing we hear is, "It wasn't my fault!" There is little or no concern for the consequences of what was done, just "How do I get myself out of this mess!" If this doesn't work, we bow our heads, produce a sheepish look and ask for forgiveness. "I'm sorry. Please forgive me." Our top priority is protecting ourselves, not confronting our fault.

Maybe this attitude stems from our predominant religious traditions. We have corrupted the idea of forgiveness and use it like a credit card we never have to repay. If we screw up, all we have to do is swipe our "I'm Sorry Card" and all is forgiven. This misuse of forgiveness is infuriating to me. Saying, "Oops!" and feeling sorry for yourself does nothing to fix what has been done. When people screw up, I expect them to honestly consider why they screwed up so that they will not screw up again. Instead of running from their mistake, they should face it head on.

I myself never apologize and I do not appreciate it when people apologize to me. If you apologize, that means you screwed up. I would much rather have you take the time to fix the thing you screwed up, instead of wasting my time listening to your sorry excuse. If the thing you did was an accident, then the apology is not necessary because you had no control over it. If the thing you did was deliberate, then you are putting me in an awkward position, and I don't like awkward positions. Here is an example:

Years ago during my days as a contractor an employee, who shall remain nameless, destroyed an expensive piece of equipment by operating the equipment while it was low on oil. This employee knew that the oil had to be checked each day, but was trying to finish up quickly so he could start his weekend early. He ran the equipment and consequently blew up the motor.

On Monday he came into the shop, hat in hand, and apologized in front of the entire crew for his mistake. Now, all of the responsibility was on me to forgive him. When I didn't accept his apology, all of the people in attendance thought that I was the most cruel person in existence. "Gee Mark, he said he was sorry", "Come on man, you could at least of accepted his apology", were just a few things I heard about this instance. But from my perspective, I was out an expensive piece of equipment, I was less one employee because I fired his ass and thirdly somehow I was the bad guy.

I do not say things that I do not mean. But, when I am angry I say things that are best left unsaid. In those situations, it doesn't do much good to apologize for true feelings. In more than 16 years of marriage to Amy, we have never had to apologize for anything that we have said or done.

Personal accountability is a thing of the past. From Corporate CEO's, to the President of the United States, to every day people, no one takes responsibility for their own actions. Child molesters are called pedophiles, because they can't help it. Drunk drivers are called alcoholics, because it's a disease. Where exactly does the buck stop? Where are the role models and people in leadership that will take responsibility for their mistakes and fix them instead of passing it off to someone else? Myself, I have no problem taking the credit for my successes, because I am the first to accept the responsibility for my failures.

It is my job to ensure things are done the right way and on time in this organization, and it is not uncommon for me to make people mad in the process. I am straight forward and sometimes a little harsh. Many people have come into my office to give me advice on the many ways I should change my tactics and personality in order to be better liked. "You catch more flies with honey" I am often told.

I don't want to catch flies, I want to rescue donkeys. So far, I have done it better than anyone else in history. I hold everyone to the same set of standards, my family especially. So if you want a pat on the head for failure, seek employment elsewhere. Want to work here? Better man-up!

Fortunately donkeys don't have toes, therefore I don't need to worry about stepping on any!

Me & Amy, or is it Amy and I?

I was going to whip an entire hockey team. I only wanted to whip one player, the guy who 2-handed me in my goalie mask with his hockey stick. But, his team intended to stand between us. I gave no thought to how many there were and the fact that my own team was no where in sight. I was going to get him and there would be hell to pay. I have an extreme temper, one that I do not lose often, but when I do…watch out. So, here I am stripping out of my goalie gear so that we could get to fighting and I heard five simple words spoken in a soft voice. Five words that had more power over me than my temper and my strong desire to punch people. What five words you ask? "Mark, get in the truck'"

The one thing I cannot do, the one power I cannot break…I cannot disappoint my wife. The thought of disappointing or embarrassing her, well that is more than I can abide. Much to the astonishment of the other team that was standing ready, I simply picked up my things and left the rink. I was still mad. I still very much wanted to punch somebody, but I was not going to hurt my wife in the process.

It is always hard to write about my family. It is very personal. I do not share personal things often. But to understand the Rescue and its success, you have to understand my relationship with my wife. Amy and I share only one absolute truth, each other. We know that no matter what, we can rely on each other. In a world where more than half of the people get divorced, this probably seems like a naïve statement, but it is our absolute truth. As sure as I am that the sun will rise in my bedroom window and the earth will be firm beneath my feet, I still put more stake in the fact that I can count on Amy.

No matter where I am, I know she will find me and come and get me. No matter how huge a task I have undertaken, I know she will stand with me. And no matter how long we are apart, I know she will wait for me. Amy knows that I will always be there as well. I will protect her, I will stand with her and will always back her, no matter what.

The Amy of today is a great deal different than the one I married. The one I married didn't want to walk down the aisle because she didn't like people looking at her. Now she is the 'She-Boss' of the entire California operation. She is smart, tough and extremely capable. She is a great mother and somehow manages to do her job as treasurer, run the California operation and still make sure our two teenage boys have her full attention.

Amy is a much better person than I am. No one will argue with that, especially me. I always try to run things by her before blurting them out. She is my reason and my conscious, two things that I sometimes lack within me. Many times, I will keep my mouth shut until I get a chance to run something by her.

My family eats, sleeps and lives animal rescue. Rescue is not what we do, it is who we are. Living with hundreds of animals, most of whom have serious problems, occupies all of our time and our every thought. With so many issues, duties, responsibilities, emergencies and so little time, it is a small wonder that so many people associated with animal rescue have a hard time keeping a significant other. Often, when only one partner is fully committed to a rescue, the other feels neglected and a they begin to drift apart.

In our own lives, Amy and I are truly happy each day. Some people find it kind of funny that we do not give each other presents. Birthdays, anniversaries and holidays pass with little notice. I was once asked if I was getting Amy flowers for Valentine's Day, to which I responded, "If I ever showed up with flowers, she would think I was cheating on her!"

In the past, Amy and I had the privilege of spending most of our time together. Meals were almost always enjoyed in each other's company. Work days, whether in the office or out with the animals, were quality time spent together. We both love our children, our grandchildren, our animals, our work and most importantly each other. Many married couples only see each other in the evenings with a little extra time on the weekends. I have even heard it said that some people never really know each other until after retirement!

Now that we have expanded our work across the country, our relationship has had to change once again. Instead of seeing each other every day, we now only get a few days each month. It is hard on both of

I think it is pretty obvious where my granddaughter Amaya gets her looks!

us, but we realize that the benefit to the rescue is incalculable. Once things settle down, we will be together on a full time basis once again.

I often reflect on the many ways that Amy and I have changed over the course of our married life. Our journey through spirituality, vegetarianism, business, education and animal rescue has always been together, step by step, hand in hand. I know I can count on her to always stand strong with me no matter how huge the challenge.

If I Die Before I Wake

I recently made the decision to euthanize my Big Dog. Big Dog was a lab mix that we adopted from a county shelter many years ago. She was on her last day and there was something about her sweet look that captured me. I knew she had been a pet, now she was just another old black dog about to be killed. Big Dog had a great life with us and she was a huge part of our family. After many years of living with diabetes, her health was in a downward spiral and she was losing her dignity, along with her quality of life. I loved that dog, but I knew I was making the right decision. This decision, while never easy, is a part of my job and one that I take very seriously.

Perhaps it is my spiritual beliefs, or more accurately my lack of spiritual beliefs, that prevent me from buying into rainbow bridges, gold paved streets and fat kids with wings and harps. Even if these things did exist, animals wouldn't be invited. When you consider the millions of cattle, chickens, pigs, dogs and cats that are killed each year, this heaven would be mighty full. Until the time that I can be shown the error in my thinking, I must make this important decision based on one truth: Dead is Dead.

If an animal's death is the end, then living must be better. But it is only better if they have quality to their lives. I use three indicators to help me make this decision:

1. Can they eat and drink on their own?
2. Can they stand and walk around?
3. Can they socialize with others of their kind?

I miss my Big Dog every day, but I know that I made the right decision. These animals rely on us for many things, things that nature would have taken care of. I can only hope that when I have no quality in my life, that I will be allowed to slip away with my dignity.

That I will be allowed to die as I lived.

Foot Note:
People often forget to leave instructions for how they would like to be treated in their last days. Here are mine:

1. *If I cannot do the "Big 3" listed above then let me go.*
2. *Play Willie, Johnny, Freddie and Stevie Ray Vaughn at my service.*
3. *Give Amy my ashes, (wait for her to die) then spread us together over the desert that I love.*
4. *If you are the least bit humane, consider cremating Larry with me.*

The Next Generation Of Me

"You don't have to be the toughest guy in the world," an old cowboy once told me, "just the toughest guy in the room." The old cowboy was Elmer Watters and I was a wide-eyed five-year-old. He lived across the street and I spent many an afternoon at his house drinking soda, eating peanuts and listening to him talk. I still remember the heavy lines on his weathered face and the way his eyes would twinkle as he told his stories. Whether he was just reliving his past or trying to prepare me for my future, I've never forgotten Elmer's wisdom.

There can be no doubt that Elmer's no-nonsense approach to life still influences how I deal with my boys. By my standards, Josh and Jake are two regular kids. But put them around other kids and the differences leap out at you. Josh and Jake have been around rescued animals almost their entire lives. Waiting to open Christmas presents until after the animals have been fed is routine. Missing a birthday dinner because a sick animal needs our attention is no big deal. Some people think that this type of life is too hard for young boys, but Amy and I think that it is the perfect way to raise two men.

I often receive letters asking to know more about Josh and Jake. I admit that this has always made me a little uncomfortable. While I'm extremely proud of them, I don't like the idea of putting them on public display. It never fails that someone, somewhere, will have something ugly to say. And, while I can take anything you can throw at me, the idea of someone criticizing my boys really gets me riled.

I tend not to share my emotions with anyone except my wife. Sometimes, however, I have to express myself in a different way, and so I write what I'm feeling. Writing helped give me a sense of closure when

we lost Clara and Ernie, and it has allowed me to express how lucky I am to have found Amy. And though I think they learn more from my actions, the time has come for me to write a few lines about my boys.

Our family is a little different than most. The boys get a hair cut at a barbershop when they get shaggy, not a fancy hairdo at a salon. When they need new clothes, they get work jeans that actually fit, not those baggy ones that might trip you up when you're being chased by a cow. And more times than not, they wear work boots and heavy work coats to school. Like most kids today, my boys carry cell phones. But you won't see them ticking away countless minutes of airtime chatting with their friends. They use them to communicate with the rest of the staff on our 100-acre ranch. To them, the cell phones are a tool, just like the pocket-knives they carry.

My boys have experienced life and death first-hand. They have witnessed suffering caused by abuse and neglect and they have discovered compassion within their own hearts. They do not count on others to solve their problems. If the water doesn't come out of the faucet, they figure out why. If the power goes out, they fire up the generator. If the animals need help, they do what needs to be done. It's true that the lifestyle of our boys builds character, but more importantly, it teaches responsibility. It builds men.

Another favorite of my old friend Elmer was, "Respect your elders, but don't take crap off anyone." My boys hold doors in public places for anyone older than themselves. They remove their hats at the dinner table. They will always greet you with a polite, "Hello!" and they will gladly help someone just because that person needs help. Sadly, this type of behavior is becoming less and less common.

Anyone mistaking their politeness as a sign of weakness, however, is in for an unpleasant surprise. My boys know their place in life and

not even a bulldozer can make them budge. Regardless of how big the problem or how menacing the adversary, they will always stand up for what is right. Being responsible for so much and having to be so self-reliant has made them tough enough to take on any challenge. I am proud of all of my children and their achievements, but the older kids are the first to tell you—Josh and Jake are special.

In these tough times of us living apart, Josh and Jake have had to take on even more responsibility. In many ways, they have had to fill my shoes and take on the man's jobs around the house. They are sensitive to Amy and her loneliness and go out of their way to pick up her spirits and keep her laughing. On top of everything else, I am pleased to say that Josh graduated from the eighth grade with more awards than any other student in his school. Jake was honored with the top musician award for being the top music student in the entire seventh grade.

I'm comforted to know that when the day comes that I am too old to lift a donkey into a trailer or throw a 120-pound bale of hay, my sons will be there to carry on my work as well as my traditions.

Looking For Answers

The deserts of the American Southwest are breathtakingly beautiful, rugged and lonely. Most people have gotten a taste of their magnificence on television, in magazines, or by driving through these regions in the comfort of their air-conditioned vehicles. The views inspire the people to ponder, "What if I were out there?"

Relatively few people venture into the desert for more than a hike or an overnight stay. Even then, they often carry a month's supply of food and water, a handheld GPS, three kinds of maps, emergency flares, rattlesnake repellant and a distress beacon. They know the hazards of the environment and want to be prepared for the worst possible scenario. If they are lucky, they will let down their guard for a few minutes and see the majesty of their surroundings before scrambling back to civilization.

As a 21st century burroman, I am no stranger to these parched, desolate places. With my donkeys, I roam the so-called wastelands. I pack as little as possible and have no room for a tent or sleeping bag. Instead, I sleep beneath a worn blanket under an even older blanket of stars. I carry just enough water to get me to the next spring, not a drop more. Make no mistake, I am aware of my surroundings and of my own limitations. It is where these two meet that I choose to venture, physically, emotionally and spiritually. I wander the land I love without society's distractions. This is the purpose of the journey — to simply be, in the here and now, alive.

There has been a good deal of speculation as to why the burroman of the past lived as he did. He survived on warm, muddy water and food so stale that even pack rats would not bother with it. His only companions

were his loyal donkeys. During the day, the merciless desert sun cast a shadow of death. At night, he slept on the rocky ground with spiders, snakes and scorpions. Even still, no one appreciated the finer things in life more than a man who survived with so little. A kiss from a woman, a good night's rest on a soft bed, and the taste of aged tequila — these things were never so sweet.

It is true that many a burroman was lured to the desert by the prospect of gold, but that is certainly not what made him stay. What was it about the land and lifestyle that held him there? It was freedom. But it was not just an escape from the rules of a society that told him where to go, how to act and what to think. It was the freedom to find answers to life's questions in his own way and in his own time. He understood that the desert possessed truths worth more than gold.

The harsh landscape challenged him to stay alive, not just from day to day, but from moment to moment. It was this precarious existence that added urgency to life's ultimate questions. Where do we come from? Where do we go? What are we supposed to do while we are here? He would scream these questions again and again into the night, only to be met with silence. And in the silence were the answers he sought, waiting to be revealed.

Most people accept the first answer they hear and stick with it. Religions have always provided their versions of the truth and for most people easy answers are the best answers. Religion gives you a formula to live by: Do this, don't do that and then you get something special. This formula seems to work well for most people, but if you ask a burroman to buy into something sight unseen, you will likely receive a colorful two-word reply. A burroman does not like being force-fed someone else's truth, so he goes looking for his own.

The trails of the desert all too often lead to a harsh existence, if not an agonizing end. Burromen have little use for pleasantries. We cuss too much. We drink too much. We will punch a friend in the jaw if he deserves to be punched. The desert teaches us to live in the moment and by the time you say, "Excuse me," the moment is gone. Yesterday has passed and a lot will still happen between now and tomorrow.

You don't have to be a desert-hardened burroman to appreciate a moment. Anyone who has ever seen a desert sunset, an eagle flying overhead or the honesty of a child's laughter, has experienced life in the moment. But these moments begin to fade as soon as they appear. We try desperately to hold on to them. We take pictures, make video recordings and tell the story over and over in the hope of immortalizing it. Still, the moment fades. Pictures do little more than preserve the memory of a memory. They can never bring the moment back.

But that's all life is—moment after moment. We were able to escape the distractions of our daily lives long enough for it to register and, by letting it go, we allow ourselves to be open for the next moment. It may not be as overwhelming as a desert sunset, as majestic as a soaring eagle or as beautiful as a child's laughter. It may, in fact, be quite ordinary—a leaf, a thunderstorm, a timeworn face. All are worthy of appreciation. These are moments, here and gone, never to return. All too often, by only seeking those grand events that punctuate our life, we fail to appreciate the smaller moments that create it.

Most of the burromen lie buried in unmarked graves, their names and faces forever lost to the living. Still, on every desert breeze drifts an answer as solemn as a last breath. If you listen carefully, you can hear it. At first, it's just a murmur. Later, it becomes a voice. And then, when you are ready, you hear your answers. I am comforted to know that I will someday join my fellow burromen and add my bones and stories to the great tale of the desert. And when the time comes, I am ready, because I have found the answers to my questions. What are the answers? That is something you have to discover for yourself, in your own way and in your own time.

Therefore the Sage desires to be desireless,
Sets no value on rare goods,
Learns to unlearn his learning,
And induces the masses to return from where they have overpassed.
He only helps all creatures to find their own nature,
But does not venture to lead them by the nose.

From the 64th Chapter of the Tao Teh Ching
Written by Lao Tzu
Translated by John C. H. Wu

Donkey Dao

When working with any animal, donkeys especially, it is important that you first remove all expectations and desires that you have regarding the outcome of your sessions. Accept that you are simply a participant, not the director. Often when our agenda is not met, we get discouraged or even angry. These feelings will not help your donkey and will build walls in your relationship instead of tearing them down.

Never ask your donkey to do something that is not in its nature. Animal tricks may seem funny, but they are a humiliating way of expressing dominance over animals. Your donkey has great potential. It is your responsibility to see that potential blossom. Some donkeys are great at pulling carts, some make great trail companions, and some like to give rides. But not all donkeys are good at everything.

Patsy has faithfully led my pack string on countless adventures in the deserts of the American Southwest. Many people are amazed to find that Patsy has no desire to pull a cart, give a ride or even spend time with me at the ranch. But once the packsaddles come out, Patsy is the first in line to go with me. This is Patsy's nature. It is not up to me to change it. It is my responsibility to see that she can express it.

All animals have their own nature. Some donkeys at the Rescue have no desire to be 'people friendly'. Because of their background, the most we can do is to offer them the opportunity to become donkeys again, nothing more, nothing less. The same is true for dogs, cats and even elephants. Often we see animals forced to perform tricks simply to amuse people. When these acts conflict with their nature, it is no wonder why some animals finally get fed up and turn on their trainers.

How do you teach a bear to ride a bike? Nail it's feet to the pedals and beat the shit out of it!
Comedian Robert Schimmel

Don't Eat My Cow &
I Won't Eat Your Dog

    I received a letter from another animal group asking for money to help stop the human consumption of dogs in Asia. I have many dogs here at the ranch and am particularly fond of two of them that travel with me everywhere I go. I could not imagine eating one of my dogs, after all, they are loving, funny, highly intelligent and seem to enjoy their life. It would seem cruel to butcher one of them and place them on the dinner table.

    Months ago, another animal group sent me a petition to stop the consumption of donkeys in Asian and European Countries. The petition went on to say that there were many other viable forms of meat readily available for consumption and why should donkeys have to suffer at some slaughter plant? After all, donkeys are loving, funny, highly intelligent and seem to enjoy their life.

    I did not support either of these two rescues on their positions. I

have two steers and one cow at my ranch in Tehachapi. I can honestly say that they are loving, funny, highly intelligent and seem to enjoy their lives. I invite everyone to come to the ranch and see this for themselves. I am not here to advocate vegetarianism, everyone is welcome to eat whatever they want. That is why we choose to live in a country where we are granted freedom. I would, however, like to question the logic behind the notion that it is acceptable for us to consume the fat, muscle, organs and fluids of one species, while the mere thought of consuming the fat, muscle, organs and fluids of another specie is abhorrent?

> Why is Angus Beef preferred to Dachshund steak?
> Why is lamb OK to eat, but puppy is not?
> Why not kitten nuggets in lieu of chicken nuggets?
> Why do we not enjoy Baby Back Ribs equally, whether they come from a pig or donkey?

This simple fact remains; companies and our government spend millions of dollars convincing people that the consumption of the fat, muscle, organs and fluids of Cattle, Sheep, Swine and Chicken is acceptable behavior. These animals do not deserve their fate any more than a Donkey, Dog or Cat. We simply make the justification in order to continue the tradition.

So in conclusion:
Don't eat my cow and I won't eat your dog..............

The Perfect Life

I think one of the reasons that Amy and I do so well together is that we are always content, regardless of where we are in life. When we were first married, we had nothing. Actually, if the truth be told, we had nothing minus twenty dollars. No matter how hard we tried, we were always twenty dollars short each week. We knew that fighting about it wouldn't change anything so we would laugh and say, "What are ya goin' to do?" And this became our motto when things didn't work the way we had hoped. We wouldn't yell at each other or lay blame, we would just laugh and say, "What are ya goin' to do?"

Too many people buy into the myth that there is a perfect place in life they must strive to find. They plead, "I would be happy if only I had," and then insert words like "a better car," "more money," "a new house," or "a new career." When they finally get to drive the right car, live in the right house, own all the right stuff and take all the right medications, they discover that happiness is still nowhere in sight. Not surprisingly, many of these people become disillusioned and bitter. This is their nightmare:

After dying, a man wakes to find himself in the house of his dreams. It has the perfect television that shows all of his favorite movies and the perfect stereo that plays all of his favorite songs. His perfect car is sitting in the driveway and his perfect mate is waiting to fulfill his every craving. He smiles and says, "Now I am finally happy."

After a period of time, however, the movies and songs get tiresome. The car is no longer fun to drive and the mate is just plain boring. So, he walks outside and screams to the sky, "I have everything I want and I can't stand it! What kind of heaven is this?"

A cruel voice then booms from all around, "You think you are in heaven? Guess again!"

The reality is that there is no perfect place in life and no amount of stuff can make us happy for very long. All we have is this moment with all of its joy and sorrow, pain and pleasure, and the simple choice to make of it what we will.

Amy and I are living our perfect life. We truly love each other and could not ask for better kids. We enjoy working together and are doing exactly what we want to be doing. We have everything we could wish for, but we have headaches, too. There are funds to raise, deadlines to meet, budgets to set, and the list goes on and on. We witness the effects of human cruelty every day and it hurts us deeply, but we also get to experience the joy that comes from calming troubled minds and mending broken bodies. At the end of the day, we take the good with the bad and keep moving forward with our mission. After all, without the lows, the highs would never amount to anything more than average.

When People Trust You

There are two major differences between my non-profit charity and the for-profit construction company I used to own. First of all, the money is not mine. When I ask someone to support the rescue, I do not receive any part of it. All funds go toward helping our animals. My paycheck remains the same small amount, even if we receive an increase in donations.

The second major difference, is that the money we receive comes from regular people. We do not get big money grants from faceless corporations or government agencies. Most people are surprised to hear that our monetary support comes from a lot of people who give little amounts. We do have a few donors who can afford to give thousands, but most donations arrive a few dollars at a time.

I received a letter many years ago from a ninety-two year old woman who lived near the Great Lakes. Ida had seen me on Animal Planet and had asked her great-granddaughter to track me down. In the letter, she told me about her children, her grandchildren, her great-grandchildren and her great-great-grandchildren. Ida went on to tell me about her childhood and the donkey she knew on the farm where she grew up. She told me about her life, her joys, her sorrows and all of the things that had led up to where she was on that very day, writing that very letter. She also included two one-dollar bills.

Now, I am not one for correspondence. If you send me an email, my response will usually be one or two lines. I'll answer your questions and that's about all. I do not mean to offend anyone, but I have my donkeys to attend to and just don't have time to write. But I was so impressed with Ida's letter that I sat down with pen and paper and wrote her back. I shared a few stories from my life and congratulated her on the loving family that she had. I also returned her two dollars. I told her that I knew she could put it to better use taking care of herself.

A week later, I received another letter from her with the two dollars and a stern scolding. While she didn't have much, she had two dollars to spare. She went on to say how she had looked in my eyes on the TV show and saw that I was an honest person who really believed in what I was saying. Ida told me that she trusted me to do what was right with the money.

I carried Ida's two dollars around with me for weeks, but just could not bring myself to part with it. There was something about those two little green pieces of paper, but what? How could a two-dollar donation affect me so much? What was I missing? When it finally hit me, it literally took my breath away. I'll never forget the moment I realized that this was more than a heartfelt donation; it was a symbol of the trust that people place in me. Money will come and go, but the trust of people like

Ida is sacred.

In a large charitable organization like ours, there are many safeguards to protect the public from fraud. We submit all of our accounting books, bank statements, cancelled checks and receipts to an independent auditor. The audit, along with our federal tax return, is posted on our website for all to see. It is also sent to our lawyer in Washington, D.C., who prepares and mails hundreds of forms along with the audit and tax return to each state's Attorney General's Office. This system protects donors and allows them to see where their money is going. Still, while the system ensures that donations are used legally, it does not ensure they are used wisely.

In order to properly care for our animals and maintain the ranch, we need to hire people, buy equipment, build structures and so on. In each case, it is my responsibility to make sure that we spend money as efficiently as possible. I have a special way of doing this. Ida and a group of imaginary little old ladies follow me everywhere I go. Every time I have to make a financial decision, I present it to my council of old ladies. Only when I feel that I can justify spending Ida's two dollars do I spend the money.

Ida and I corresponded back and forth for almost six months when one day I received a letter from her son saying that Ida had passed away. He thanked me for giving his mother a bright spot in her day when she could open her letter from me and read to all who would listen. I miss writing those letters, but I will always have Ida standing beside me as I make this rescue live on.

Foot Note:

I was recently asked by someone, who read the second edition, if I still had Ida's two dollars in my wallet. I must admit that I spent those two dollars, but it was not really my fault. Amy and I were travelling along the coast of California on our way to pick up some donkeys when Amy said, "there is a donkey laying down back there and it looks like he was in two feet of manure."

We turned around and sure enough, here was a donkey with painfully long hooves and a crooked leg laying in a tiny pen filled with manure. I knocked on the door and told the man who answered that I would like buy his donkey for twenty dollars. The man abruptly slammed the door in my face. I said loudly though the door, "I am not leaving here with out that donkey, either talk to me or talk to the police."

The man opened the door and said, "That donkey's worth a lot more than twenty dollars."

I explained that I only had twenty on me but he would not get a nickle if I filed a complaint with the authorities. Seeing the signs on the truck and trailer, he became a little more congenial, "let me see your wallet, I bet you got more than twenty."

  I opened my wallet to him and showed the wallet's contents, exactly one twenty dollar bill. "What about those" he said seeing the edges of Ida's two one dollar bills, stuck behind my organ donor card.
  "They're yours" I said without hesitation, "but I am taking the donkey and we are done negotiating."
  And for twenty two dollars we were able to bring Roger home and finally spend Ida's money.

```
Products Named Zen, Seldom Are
```

In Western society, we have been programmed to always be one step ahead. When our alarm goes off, we are already thinking about our first cup of coffee. As we are drinking our coffee, we are reading the newspaper. As we are commuting, we think about our workload. As soon as we get to work, we are thinking about lunch. At lunch, we are thinking about what we will watch on television later that night.

We, as a society, are seldom present in the moment. We are never just eating, just driving, just working. When was the last time you saw a car without a radio or a home without a television? We are never alone and just being quiet. With so many distractions, how can we find ourselves amidst all of the hustle and bustle?

When I am with animals, I am simply with animals. I do not think of anything. I do not let distractions lead me away from just being there with my friends. It sounds simple enough, but actually putting it into practice can be difficult. How many of us have phones that follow us everywhere? When we settle into our 'time off', how many of us see things that need to be repaired?

Zen is the practice of being present in the moment. Regardless of our religious, spiritual or cultural beliefs, all of us should try to be 'Zen' once in awhile. Taking the opportunity to be present in the moment when you are with your animals is truly an enriching experience. By focusing and not being distracted by extraneous thoughts, you will learn things that you never before noticed. You will discover small things about yourself and your animals that will create a lasting bond. You will hear sounds, see small gestures and learn the nature of yourself, your animals, and the world around you.

I have spent hours upon hours just being with my herd of donkeys. Not being involved, just being present. It is these experiences that have taught me the "whys" and "hows" of their behavior.

There is an old Indian legend that says when a man dies he must cross a bridge into the afterlife. At the head of this bridge waits every animal that he encountered during his lifetime. The animals decide which of us can cross and which are turned away.

www.donkeyrescue.org

The Dead Bridge

I used to end my speaking engagements with an exercise that I learned from a Buddhist monk. I would guide my audience through an examination of their lifestyle and the ways in which they unwittingly contribute to the world's problems. "This does not make you a bad person," I would say, "but now that you are aware, you can take responsibility for your actions." At worst, most people consider themselves apathetic bystanders, but if forced to look more closely, they see that everything they do affects everything else on the planet. There are no sidelines and, like it or not, everyone is in the game.

I have since learned that it is useless, not to mention unpopular, to point out the faults of others with the hope of changing their lifestyle. People will desperately cling to destructive beliefs and habits rather than take a single step into the unknown. Like my donkeys, people must decide for themselves when it is right for them to move forward. And when that time comes, each individual must find his or her own way. But where do you start?

On the wall of my office is a picture of three donkeys standing in a large field. I really like the picture and will often catch myself staring at it. At the bottom of the picture is this saying:

"There is an old Indian legend that says, when a man dies, he must cross a bridge into the the afterlife. At the head of this bridge waits every animal that he encountered during his lifetime. The animals decide which of us can cross and which are turned away."

In my life, I have been far from perfect. I have not always rescued animals or been a vegetarian. I have not always shown patience or kindness to fellow humans. I have often used my strengths to gain an advantage over those who were not as smart, strong, or resourceful. In fact, I became so good at taking that society gave me a label: successful.

The point of the above saying is not whether an animal bridge really exists, but how we see ourselves through the eyes of others. And these others are not our bosses, our leaders or even our gods, but rather the weak, the overlooked and those who are taken for granted. In our own honest opinion, if we can measure up in their eyes, then maybe we are doing something right after all.

I have often asked myself, "Would I be allowed to cross the bridge?" I now live a life in which I give more than I take. I may no longer be considered a success by others, but I know that if such a bridge did exist, my sweet little Clara would be waiting to lead me hand in hoof to the other side.

Who will you face at your bridge? It is never too late to change.

Part 4
MY SCRAPBOOK

     This section contains some of my pictures, artwork and graphics that I couldn't fit in anywhere else. A big part of our work is to try and show donkeys, as well as the other animals, in a new light. I hope that by seeing the donkeys differently, people will not be so quick to write them off.

     While I realize that I am not a professional photographer or graphic designer, I take a lot of pride in the fact that my photographs and graphic designs have been seen by hundreds of thousands of people worldwide. It just goes to show that round pegs do not have to fit into square holes, we just need to be tough enough to make the holes fit us.

     Many of these works can be purchased as posters and prints through our online gift store. Please send us an email if there is something not listed that you are interested in. As with all of my work, all proceeds benefit the donkeys. Please visit www.donkeyrescue.com

Go Green! it's good for you, me & the planet

Conserve
Recycle
Reuse

visit www.donkeyrescue.org to learn more

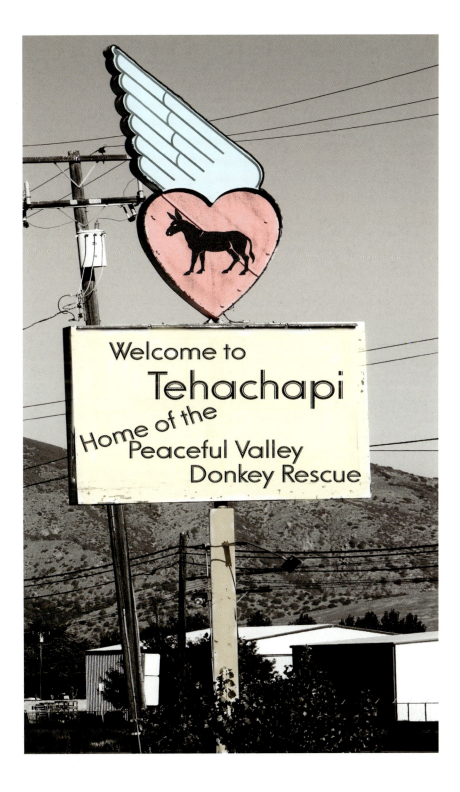

Part 5
WRAPPING UP

> Every day I looked in the mirror and said "I am not crazy"
>
> *Don Ameche*
> *from Harry and the Hendersons*

Every once in awhile, I question my own sanity and the sacrifice that my family and I have made to bring this dream into a reality. Usually it stems from loneliness or regret because I have once again missed something important back home. I am usually able to remind myself that this quest, when finished, will have been worth it.

For me, rescuing donkeys has always come easy. It is the dealing with government civil servants who mistakenly think they have some measure of control over me and insurance companies that cannot embrace anything outside of their perfect little box of existence that make my job so difficult.

I have my dogs for company on the long trips and the evenings. The donkeys and the Rescue to occupy my days. But in the waning moments of my life, it will be the time away from my family that I will lament. Everyone else was either an ally or an obstacle.

As this book goes to pre-press in early Fall 2008, I am told that we are once again needed in Northern Nevada to remove excess burros on Federal Lands. I'll start packing soon, the battle rages on.

I hope you have enjoyed Talking With Donkeys.   MSM

Book Signing Event

     Talking With Donkeys Editions 1 and 2 have brought in a combined revenue of over $50,000 to the Rescue. Not too bad for a bunch of stupid, stubborn and dangerous donkeys and a guy who quit paying attention in the 6th grade and doesn't play well with others!

Foot Note: The more books you buy, the more donkeys we can rescue.
So buy more books!
www.donkeyrescue.com

Glossary of Terms

Alfalfa: Hay that was designed for milk cows and should never be fed to donkeys. Never, never! Problems such as obesity and hoof deterioration can result.

Wild Ass: An endangered species and the rootstock for the burros of the New World.

Bray: The distinctive Hee-Haw of the donkey, creating sound on the inhale and exhale.

Burro: The Spanish word for Ass; usually referring to wild animals.

Burroman: The last of a forgotten breed. A man who draws a hard line.

Donkey: The English word for Ass; usually referring to domestic animals. "Dun" meaning gray and "ky" meaning diminutive. A small gray animal.

Equine: Any member of the horse family, i.e. donkey, horse, zebra, mule.

Farrier: Professional that trims and shoes equine hooves.

Feral: Term used to describe any non-indigenous animal.

Flehmen: Raising of the top lip in order to gather scent in the roof of the mouth. Also "flehming".

Floating: The act of grinding off sharp edges of teeth.

Founder: The deterioration of the bone within the hoof; usually caused by an improper diet of alfalfa and oats; extremely painful.

Grass Hay: Hay that is the closest match to a donkey's natural diet. It comes in many forms, including Bermuda, Timothy, Orchard and Bromegrass.

Hinny: The hybrid offspring of a male horse and female donkey; usually more horse-like.

Jack: A male donkey.

Jennet: A female donkey; also referred to as Jenny.
John: A male mule.

Laminitis: The deterioration of the lamina or lining between the hoof and the bone within the hoof wall; usually caused by improper diet or abnormal stress to the body.

Mammoth: Donkeys that stand 56" or more at the withers.

Miniature: Donkey that stand 36" or less at the withers.

Molly: A female mule.

Mule: The hybrid offspring of a male donkey and female horse. It can be bred from miniature to mammoth but is nearly always sterile and unable to reproduce.

Pannier: Pack bags used to carry equipment. Also "panyard".

Parasite: Internal worms that cause serious health problems; controlled with a worming regimen given every 3 months. Parasites can be external or internal.

Sawbuck: A traditional pack saddle made from wood.

Standard: Donkeys measuring between 36" and 54" at the withers.

Sully: A term used to describe a donkey that will "shut down" to avoid the pain associated with prolonged abuse.

Withers: The "shoulders" - the highest part of the back, height is determined at the withers.

About The Author

Mark Meyers is Executive Director of Peaceful Valley, which has five divisions, covering animal welfare from animal rescue to educational programs. Mark also serves as Chairman of Peaceful Valley's Board of Trustees and oversees the National Operations of the Donkey Rescue.

Mark Meyers has been seen on television programs around the world. He has also been a guest on several radio programs and authored several books and articles. His public speaking engagements include business organizations, service clubs and classrooms ranging from the kindergarten to university level. Mark brings his lively desert adventures, heartwarming rescue stories and living philosophy of compassion everywhere he goes.

His work at the Rescue, as well as his adventures with his donkeys in the deserts of America, have been featured in:

Animal Planet's "Wild Rescues"
Animal Planet's "That's My Baby"
Animal Planet's "Adoption Tales"
Animal Planet's "Animal Icons"
Animal Planet's "BH Vet"
Fox TV's "Animal Miracle"
Per Erik Eriksson's Documentary "Bad Ass"
Per Erik Eriksson's Documentary "Haulin' Ass Up Panamint Mountain"
San Francisco's Evening News
Antelope Valley Magazine
The Los Angeles Times
The Antelope Valley Press
The Bakersfield Californian
The Country Journal
The Antelope Valley Magazine Hero Edition
The Brayer Magazine
New England's "Creature Corners"
The SF Bay Area's "Galloping Gazette"
and countlesss others that have publshed his works.

Mark's TV Shows are available on DVD through the Peaceful Valley Gift Shop, please visit www.donkeyrescue.com

Acknowledgements

I would like to thank the following people:

All of the Burromen of old, especially Pete Aguereberry, Shorty Harris, Smitty, Walter Scott and Burro Bill for their stories, legends and love of the desert. Without them, I would never have found my way around the desert or my own path in life.

Willie Nelson for his music. While I have never met Mr. Nelson, his songs and my poor excuse for a singing voice have kept the donkeys entertained on many a desert adventure.

Kinky Friedman for sharing his time, wisdom and humor.

The Peaceful Valley Trustees, Staff, Satellite Operators, Donors, Volunteers and everyone else who works so hard to make the Peaceful Valley Donkey Rescue such a huge success.

John and Kevin for always having my back. Whether we are conquering mountains or fighting evil, I can always count on them.

Devin for being a believer and helping to roll the giant rock.

Joshua and Jacob Meyers for being mature and dependable, way beyond their years.

And my dearest wife Amy, for always being there to save me from the desert, from Deming and especially from myself.

I would also like to thank the people that have shown so much love and support to me, my family and the Rescue:
Gary and Donna Meyers, Shelly, Tood & Amaya Deguchi, Ivy, Steven Meyers, Jan Blumentritt and Charles Sponsel, Frank and Vicky Dydek, Chris and Gina Lea, Lisa and Brian Depuy, Gary and Julie Wiseman, Robert and Gale Seddon, Art Schaefer
and, of course, Larry.

Contact Information

Peaceful Valley Donkey Rescue
PO Box 2210
Tehachapi, CA 93581
Phone 661-822-3953
www.donkeyrescue.org
info@donkeyrescue.org

Texas Burro Rescue
PO Box 216
Miles, TX 76861
Phone 325-468-4123
www.texasburros.org
info@texasburros.org

Talking With Donkeys
www.talkingwithdonkeys.com
order copies online at: www.donkeyrescue.com

Watch the Peaceful Valley Team in action at
www.pvdr247.com

In my career as a rescuer, I have made three simple promises:
1. I will improve the Plight of the American Donkey.
2. I will be a part of something bigger than myself.
3. I will not allow my cause to die with me.

    I have tried to heed JB Wise and never settle for second. I have remembered Elmer and never been the toughest guy in the world, just the toughest one in the room. And while I may not be remembered as the most popular, I can honestly say that my intentions were pure.
    When I am gone, I do not want a marble tribute in a grassy field recalling my name and dates. Nor would I appreciate a roadside memorial of candles and crosses. And I am not at all interested in having my name on a stadium, building or freeway.
    All I hope for is that my memory will be passed on as my story is repeated in the brays, barks and various other sounds of the animals whose lives I was fortunate enough to have been a part of.

Mark Meyers
A Simple Burroman
1964-